THE NAFALLEN UNIVERSITY COURSE CATALOG

EDITED BY MATT HENSHAW AND JOHN BALTISBERGER

Madness Heart Press
2006 Idlewilde Run Dr.
Austin, Texas 78744

Cover by John Baltisberger
Interior Layout by Lori Michelle
      www.TheAuthorsAlley.com

For more information, address:
      john@madnessheart.press

www.madnessheart.press

DEPARTMENTS

Editor's note: Collected herein are the extant course descriptions from the latest Nafallen University Course Catalog. Courses referenced in Prerequisites but not visible in this catalog do indeed exist, but are only accessible after tuition payment has been made.

AGRICULTURE

Thank you for your interest in our department's offerings. Through our undergraduate coursework, we hope to provide to the serious student a thorough and intensive education of plants, fungi, and their relationship to the planet, humanity, and our Masters who we aim to welcome through the diaphanous veil between our dimensions. Our small but dedicated faculty has extensive and esoteric knowledge that is unique to Nafallen. We eagerly await you in our classes, in our fields.

NAFALLEN UNIVERSITY

AGR 101: True Groundwork (Proper Preparation of Agricultural Cornfields and Meadowlands for Disparate Large-scale Rituals) —Soil Studies I
Prerequisites: None

An offering to the great Masters is only as good as the crops that have been raised. And those are only as good as the soil in which those crops were seeded. In this introductory survey, students will discover the proper elements of good and true groundwork. Analysis of soil samples from Koombs farm will yield wondrous revelations which will spur the inspired students on in their agricultural studies.

AGR 161: Fungal Studies I
Prerequisites: None (AGR 101 recommended prior or concurrent)

A 12-week course of study of Fungi on this planet, a history of cultivation and uses throughout time both past and future.

AGR 179: Animal Husbandry (and Its Intersection with Arcane and Esoteric Liturgical practices)
Prerequisites: AGR 101: True Groundwork (Proper Preparation of Agricultural Cornfields and Meadowlands for Disparate Large-scale Rituals)

Techniques learned via lectures and group study include guidelines for accurate incantations to transform goats into mystic familiars, proper examination of sheep and lambs for wens and blemishes prior to ritual sacrifice, and nuances of cattle hide inversion to ensure correct placement in crop circles.

Progress will be determined by several unscheduled quizzes and a comprehensive final that will require students to detail three main themes of the course textbook using an expository outline format. A field trip to Koombs Farm, west of Crisp, Texas for in-depth study of various topics may be arranged for extra credit.

Required Textbook: "The Book of the Bred—Eldritch Uses of Livestock" by Alfred Al-Hazred

AGR 181: Chlorophyllosophy
Prerequisites: Permission from the instructor pending written application

In this course, students will investigate the nature of chlorophyll—its origins and its adversarial relationship with the fungal kingdom. By the end of the course, students can expect to have the knowledge to combat the lie that chlorophyll is necessary for life on this planet (or this universe), and in fact, is a detriment to ultimate existence.

AGR 201: Intro to Grand Agricultural Practice
Prerequisites: AGR 101, AGR 161, and AGR 181 recommended-admission permitted upon review and acceptance of written application

In this course, the student is introduced into the concepts and philosophies of Grand Agricultural Practice. Why do humans grow things? Why are plants lesser than fungi? How may Grand Agricultural Practice help to evolve the human race, and bring us in congress with Those Who Came Before and Will Rise to Rule Us Once Again? In addition to lecture hours, students are expected to work a minimum of 12 hours during the semester on the Koombs Farm annex to pass the course and proceed into further study.

AGR 222: Soil Studies II—Botanical Food Quality
Prerequisites: BIO 129: Introduction to Human Nutritional Sciences

A guided examination of individual life and health choices, with the goal of ensuring that every future corpse is able to provide local fungal life with the most nutrient-rich loam possible.

AGR 261: Fungal Studies II
Prerequisites: AGR 101, AGR 161

Continued studies of the fungal kingdom, including but not limited to methods of growth, correct harvest techniques, and basic Mycorrhizal network theory and application. Labs to be performed on the Koombs Farm annex.

AGR 271: Mycorrhizal Networks
Prerequisites: AGR 261

A more intensive course focusing on Mycorrhizal networks, and how they can be utilized for our Grand Agricultural Practice. Students will tap into mycelium in the local forest system to explore how the fungi communicate with one another, and with those who lurk, waiting, beyond our dimension. Labs to be performed on the Koombs Farm annex and the adjacent Tymothee Forest Preserve.

AGR 291: Fungal Sentience and Grand Agricultural Practice
Prerequisites: AGR 271

Building upon the Prerequisites course work, the student will now marry the concepts of mycorrhizal networks with the basic concepts of Grand Agricultural Practice to begin more advanced studies of the true cosmic nature of agriculture. 50% of student course time will be spent on site at the Koombs Farm annex, though we expect you will want to spend more time than that on the grounds.

AGR 301: Grand Agricultural Practice and You
Prerequisites: AGR 291

You have worked on the farm, harvesting the various fungi, fertilizing the land with your toilsweat and, perhaps, a little blood (and maybe an unnecessary digit from your left hand). The mycelium sing a dark lullaby to you in the wee hours of the morning. You learn best in the dark, bare feet in cool black soil. Now, in AGR 301, learn more advanced secrets of how to raise a truly colossal and welcomed crop. Students will complete the course ready to step over the threshold from Grand Agricultural Practice into TRUE AGRICULTURE. Minimum of 30 hours per week spent on site at Koombs Farm annex.

AGR 351: Intro to TRUE AGRICULTURE
Prerequisites: Admission to TRUE AGRICULTURE certificate program per review by Prof. Koombs and faculty committee

So Called "Farming" has become a new f-word obscenity to you now that you are pursuing your certificate in TRUE AGRICULTURE. Those so called "F-rm-rs" have no conception of the awe-full beauty that you are ready to embark upon bringing into this world. In this Introduction to TRUE AGRICULTURE, students will separate the proverbial wheat from the chaff, and cultivate new advanced practices in fungal communication, using the hyphae to foster not just human-fungal communication, but to begin to understand direction from Those For Whom We Grow. Attendance at Koombs Farm annex is strictly enforced-more than 2 absences will result in expulsion from the program at the hands of advanced agricultural adepts.

AGR 361: TRUE AGRICULTURE II
Prerequisites: AGR 351 and minimum 300 hours service at Koombs Farm annex.

The penultimate course work in TRUE AGRICULTURE certification, the fungi are the faculty now, and they have so much to teach you. It is dawning on you that you are the field to be tended, cultivated, and ultimately harvested. The farm is all-consuming for you now, the outside world meaningless. Ultimately, even the farm will be insignificant in the grand course of things. Those For Whom We Grow are pleased with your progress, and begin to share their plans, which you will gladly be a part of. Which we will all be a part of. Grow children grow, and prepare to take the final steps.

AGR 401: Practicum in TRUE AGRICULTURE
Prerequisites: Faculty review and acceptance of practicum content

Rejoice for the time is nigh! At completion of this practicum, you have earned certification in TRUE AGRICULTURE. Those For Whom We Grow will direct you in your independent work. You will listen, and nothing will matter more to you than successfully manifesting their ideas. It is time for the Great Harvest, and for the cycle to begin again. Your studies complete, it is time to put all the previously learned concepts into physical practice. In addition to projects, students taking AGR 401 may be asked to weed out underperforming students by the faculty. You will not refuse and be glad in your work.

BUSINESS

At Nafallen University, we take business very seriously. Through a degree program in business, students will be prepared to understand what goods need to be exchanged for what services, the negotiating process, and most importantly, sealing the deal in blood, sweat, and tears.

NAFALLEN UNIVERSITY

BUS 101: Monetizing Your Monstrosity
Prerequisites: None

Wondering if you could rent out your monstrous creation for profit? Or if you could monetize your leftover corpses? The foundational course for business majors, students will explore questions like these, develop a full line of products and services, and write a complete business plan. This course contains everything you need to get your business off (or under) the ground.

BUS 102: Manipulating Markets
Prerequisites: BUS 101 or professor approval?

Funding subversive activity can be costly; therefore, in this elective business course, students will learn how global markets work, and how they can work for them. This course provides real-time experience in manipulating world markets for personal gain. Begin amassing your personal wealth now so that as a graduate of Nafallen University, you can focus on the important work the Masters compel you to do, what you really love doing.

BUS 107—Negotiating for Artifacts

Artifacts are a key component in any student's success. Useful in scientific study, ritual, and fashion, artifacts are a cornerstone for all business transactions. Because of this high demand, it is an undeniable truth that those with the artifacts will always be in a position of power over those who desire them. In this course, we will discuss how to overcome this, and what methods may be used to secure artifacts when traditional deals and negotiation fall short.

BUS 121: Beyond Money Laundering
Prerequisites: None

Whether to defraud social welfare programs, avoid being taxed on your weapon collection and grave digging equipment, or keep the evidence away from the authorities, this course will teach you how to effectively commingle or completely hide your fixed assets.

BUS 123: Fundamentals of Social Engineering
Prerequisites: None

This workshop-style course teaches how to use psychological concepts to manipulate, deceive, and/or gain entry into places where you are unwanted. Start small by learning how to influence humans to give you information without even knowing they have. Then work up to manipulating small and large groups of people. This course is perfect for vampires in need of invitations, identity thieves, and budding politicians.

BUS 161: Covert Advertising
Prerequisites: BUS 123: Fundamentals of Social Engineering

In this course, students will learn how to effectively advertise their assassination or theft services by identifying an existing target market or creating a new one, connecting their market with well-trained sales representatives, and developing mechanisms for repeat business from a loyal customer base without earning the attention of authorities. All students will hone their skills while interning with an existing assassination business. Note: This course requires a signed liability waiver. Nafallen University is not responsible for any physical or mental harm that occurs as a result of students' internship.

BUS 203—Navigating The Market, Both Wet and Black

Often a business need will arise that can't be attained legally, or through moral channels. In these cases, the enterprising individual must turn towards mercenaries, smugglers or the elusive Black Markets. The problem with both the Black and Wet market is that the murky legality of these market places are rife pitfalls. In this class the student will learn how to avoid these dangers and make a killing at the same time.

BUS 221: Finding and Exploiting Your Sycophants
Prerequisites: BUS 123 and BUS 161

To really make it in the business world, it is essential to be surrounded by people who will not stand in your way. This course will teach students how to build a team of yes-persons around them through a careful screening process. Once the sycophants are assembled, the student will then learn how to exploit their personal weaknesses and need for approval to both make them look better, as well as foster jealousy and in-fighting between them. Guest C-Suite speakers will present special sessions throughout the semester.

BUS 301: Advanced Resume and Cover Letter Techniques
Prerequisites: ENL 160 and BUS 221 recommended

This advanced course in Resume and Cover Letter Techniques is split into two halves. In the first half, students will apply the Bartlett Method to use carefully selected words in a certain order to catch the attention of a potential employer and convince them that you are the right person for the job. Then, in the second half, students will learn to look for saccadic elements in letters and resumes to recognize both familiars and potential nemeses.

BUS 381: The Accursed
Prerequisites: At least 9 credit hours of prior BUS courses.

This course examines the general economy based on consumption and expenditure. Students will participate in decadent feasts, orgies, and human sacrifice to explore the flow of excess energy into waste.

BUS 433: Nihilism in Business
Prerequisites: 9 credit hours of BUS coursework

At the end of the day, business ventures are bound to fail, either due to the unpredictable nature of the marketplace, changes in taste, or eradication of cultures and populations. It is important in business to plan for these eventualities, and ensure a precious-metal parachute is ready so that you can land with security while your underlings are left to clean up the mess and serve time for criminal malfeasance. In this course, students will be cleared of any lingering ideas that *what* their business plan might be *actually* matters in any ultimate sense.

COMMUNICATION

Communication is said to exist only between equals. While there is no equivalency that can be drawn between humankind and the Masters, you will learn the tools necessary to communicate their Will to your peers and underlings.

NAFALLEN UNIVERSITY

COM 102: Intro to Mediumship
Prerequisites: None

In this freshman level course, students are taught the basics of mediumship (communicating with the dead) in practice, as well as the history of the practice and how its rituals have evolved over the years.

COM 103: Building Core Networks

This Communications elective focuses on the importance of building social networks across diverse populations discreetly. Make connections within and beyond the classroom to build a core network for yourself. Learn what core resources other disciplines require for their work, and how they refer to them (publicly and privately). Perhaps you enjoy the act of wet work but hate the disposal aspect: a liar's bones, a cancerous mass, entrails and other parts are all coveted ingredients for certain practitioners. At course completion students will be granted access to the University's alumni intranet. The Communication department recommends taking this course concurrently with COM 312.

COM 202: Advanced Mediumship
Prerequisites: Successful completion of COM 102 or Instructor Approval

The second course in this sequence focuses more on the specific rituals unique to mediumship, with attention given to the students own successful practice of mediumship as a requirement for successful completion of the course.

COM 312: Dastardly Diction

In this course, students will master diction to disguise their dastardly and delicious deeds. Learn common slang and jargon as well as industry-standard code language for violent acts so that they may be better shared and celebrated in public settings. The Communication department recommends taking this course concurrently with COM 103.

COM 315: Pattern Recognition and Application in Communications
Prerequisites: Successful completion of 100 or 200 Level Communication Course(s)

Being able to translate and understand different languages is an entirely different skill than being able to translate what is *not* said. When what is being asked for is occluded in the patterns between and *within* the words. Beyond even the etymologies and the cultures behind the language, being able to hone in on these patterns will lead to great success in Communications. Students taking this course will learn to identify and respond to these patterns accordingly to lead inexorably towards the desired Outcomes.

COM 326: Necromancy
Prerequisites: Junior standing; Successful completion of Comm 103 & 203

In this two-semester course, students will learn the history of the practice as well as the more successful rituals meant to succeed at the practice of necromancy (the raising of the dead). Students will study the biographies of the more successful necromancers throughout history, and will finally complete a necromancy ritual meant to raise the corpse of their choice with instructor approval.

COM 405: Forbidden Speech
Prerequisites: A willingness to tear your tongue out at the root.

For the student of great mental fortitude, speaking with eternity itself is the ultimate goal. This course will teach speech so beautiful, the human mouth cannot properly articulate it in its current state. The transformation of the student's mouth and throat will be excruciating, but the reward will be full of wonder.

COM 433: Summoning the Eldritch Gods
Prerequisites: Senior Standing + Outstanding Practicum Scores , PHL 403: Ethics of Ritual and Summoning

Summoning the Eldritch Gods requires great patience and an understanding that practitioners can't control the Gods, but merely beseech them for assistance. This seminar is meant to introduce students to the rituals deemed most successful by practicing sorcerers.

COMPUTER SCIENCE

In the last century, no human innovation has resulted in more change than the invention of the computer. Indeed, the power computers wield is unprecedented to the average person. As a student taking Computer Science at Nafallen University, you will come to appreciate and be in thrall to that power. For the student who excels in their studies, they will discover that with a few keystrokes they have the potential to serve the will of the Masters well.

CSC 044: Unreasonably Complex Build Systems

Don't make it easy for other people to build and run your scientific software. After all, real science is not for fools, commoners, or the faint of heart. In this elective, we will discuss obscure compiler flags, version dependent features of the "make" and "gcc" commands, and how to write code that depends upon them. We will explore the art of using multiple scripting languages at once for code generation. Using a logic analyzer, we are able to prove the final system is comprehensible only by individuals who conform to a diagnosis of schizophrenia according to the DSM-VI.

CSC 101: Goetic Programming
Prerequisites: Hermetic Calculus recommended

This course introduces the student to metaphysical data abstraction by studying the concepts of Goetic materialization, Clavicular algorithmic buildout, Theosophical research and design, and coding and testing using an Enochian software development environment. Topics include analysis of early Solomonic texts, fundamentals of evocation control structures, Kabbalistic arrays, multidimensional Boolean logic, and Astral Projection Array (APA) procedures. Applicants must be comfortable with using ichor (human or otherwise) for ritualistic permutations. Basic knowledge of Deep Mandaic is also necessary to communicate with the disembodied thought-forms residing in the higher plane of Malkuth. Weekly laboratory experiments involving personal bloodletting and flesh-sculpting will prepare undergraduates for a doctorate course in machine learning and automation of biomechanical constructs such as golems, hypogogglian entities, and reanimated corpses. Successful learners will have multiple eyes grafted on the surface of their cerebral cortexes upon receiving a final course grade of B++ or above.

CSC 116: Metaphysical Cryptography
Prerequisites: CSC 101

Designed for students with no security experience or background, CSC 116 covers basic cryptographic terminology and concepts. This course introduces applicants to multiversal breach management, psionic networking, and metaphysical forensic analysis. Learning goals include describing the use of wireless cerebral clusters in a security context, identifying structural hemorrhaging in the fabric of the known universe, and researching failed attempts at hostile extradimensional takeovers by malicious actors. Applicants must have a grade of B++ or higher from CSC 101 to be successful. Daily learning activities involve:

- Breaching the blood-brain barrier of various alien life-forms dwelling within advanced intergalactic civilizations.
- Complete possession of xenomorphic test subjects.
- Creating psychic wounds to be utilized as backdoors for ease of access.

CSC 116 will equip learners with the necessary skills for potential careers within corporate security or military intelligence. Undergraduates with consistent grades of A or above have interned at the Groom Lake research facility in Nevada for further training in remote viewing, planar intrusion, and reality manipulation. For more information on possible job opportunities after graduation, please view "The Men Who Stare at Goats" DVD at the Bross Memorial Media Library on Campus. Though satirical, the events in this movie are based on the exploits of famed alumnus Guy Savelli.

CSC 149—Intro to Coding Syntax
Prerequisites—None

In this course, entry level students in the Computer Science program will look at programming languages FORTRAN, C#, and BASIC and investigate the esoteric commonalities of their design and syntax. Students will then apply these commonalities to other languages such as SQL, Python, and C++, and devise software which will permit entities egress to source codes utilized by federal, state, and local government databases.

CSC 249—Advanced Coding Syntax
Prerequisites—Passing score in CSC 149

In advanced Coding Syntax, the student will build upon the knowledge gained in CSC 149, and expand to a host of uncommon programming languages, including but not limited to: GYFPOL, Beolian, JAG*, Orangavac, and others. Through diligent study fueled by caffeine and other nootropics deep into the wee hours of the morning, students will apply programs written in these languages to online gaming platforms of their choosing. Students will marvel at the results of the work, both in the virtual gaming space as well as the meat space.

CSC 400—Practicum—Computing Language Creation
Prerequisites—Abstract and Code sample submitted to Dean of Computer Science for review and approval.

Taking all the student has learned in their previous coursework, this practicum will serve as the proving ground for the Senior student programmer's mettle. After acceptance of an abstract and code sample by the Dean, the student will then be granted mainframe access to NORAD servers to do their testing. This capstone project should at a minimum elicit a Defcon 3 level event with at least three other nation-states.

NOTE: Applications involving playing a game of thermonuclear war will be summarily rejected.

ENGINEERING

Making the world a more suitable place for the Masters through engineering science. Attain the skillset necessary to make this dimension a more pleasing one for the Masters and their denizens. This department is grateful for the underwriting and support of Robbins Raising Company.

EGR 110: Foundations in Engineering
Prerequisites: Passing scores in High School Science

Students taking Foundations in Engineering will learn of the literal foundational laws which allow for structures to be erected, standing, and torn down. Guest speakers from the Robbins Raising Company will present on their jobs in engineering and potential job opportunities awaiting graduates of the engineering degree program.

EGR 150: Demolition Principles I
Prerequisites: EGR 110

This lab-intensive class in Demolition Principles will explore the ways and means to eradicate a variety of architectural eyesores. Through both physical and virtual modeling, students will become experts at identifying the weakest points of any structure and how to best exploit them for maximum destruction. Students attaining a passing score may be considered for unpaid intern work at Robbins Raising Company.

EGR 185: Basic Biorobotics
Prerequisites: EGR 110

Students in EGR 185 will learn how to combine the biological with the mechanical in an unholy and uncanny replication of life. Harness the frightening and awesome power of electricity and incorporate it into the raw material of a freshly killed mole, squirrel, or rabbit to grant it new life.

EGR 181: Cyclopean Architecture
Prerequisites: Must have passport, updated inoculations, willing to travel

In this course, students will learn the basics of non-Euclidean architecture, how to measure unseeable, arcane angles, investigate the nature of Hypogogglian construction techniques, and modern-day applications. Basic sanity and mental anguish protection strategies will be offered and employed for the duration of the course. By the end of the course, students can expect to have the knowledge to measure architecture that spans more than three dimensions, understand the relationship between arcane building codes and Great Old One response and communication.

NOTES:
1. Students will be expected to own or purchase protective equipment and weaponry. While not expected, preparations must be made in case of hypogogglian encounters.
2. Students will be expected to own or purchase measurement tools compatible with up to 11 dimensions.
3. Extreme cold weather gear strongly suggested.
4. Liability waivers must be signed and returned by end of first class.

EGR 210: Non-Euclidean Architecture
Prerequisites: 100-level Mathematics course recommended. Not recommended for those with disorders of the inner ear as balance is crucial when rendering extradimensional spaces.

Upon completion of this course, students will be able to apply everything they've learned about Non-Euclidean Mathematics to design and construct otherworldly structures right here on Earth. Work internships (unpaid) at The Robbins Raising Company are available to gain industry experience.

EGR 250: Demolition Principles II
Prerequisites: EGR 150

Students who have demonstrated aptitude through coursework in EGR 150 will find EGR 250 a welcome challenge. In this progressive course on Demolition Principles, students will widen their destructive palette to more than just common structures and buildings. Using techniques ranging from the Carter Calculation to methods *we cannot include in this listing*, no structure by man or nature will stand if it is your (and the Masters') Will that it does not.

EGR 385: Advanced Biorobotics
Prerequisites: EGR 185: Basic Biorobotics

For the student who has mastered the science of using steel and electricity to reanimate the corpses of animals, this course will continue to applying these techniques to the corpses of humans. Students will not only learn to bring the rotted cadaver back to life, but to manipulate the meat puppet to perform labor and deny it the eternal sleep.

EGR 401: Acoustic Enigmas
Prerequisites: Consultation with Dr. Riley (includes an intensive hearing test and psychological assessment)

This course is designed for engineering majors who have an interest in the science of Acoustics. Guest lecturer, Dr. Elizabeth Riley, Professor Emeritus, Department of Acoustics, University of Wimburshire, England, will organize students into five different teams. Each team is assigned to one of five unique acoustic enigmas; the Hum, Skyquakes, the Siberian Hell Hole, the Upsweep, and Colossi Memnon. Teams will examine existing recordings and data and seek out new ways and methods to communicate with or connect to the source of these sounds and signals.

Disclaimer: Nafallen University is not responsible for any injury, demonic possession, misophonia, loss of mind, loss of hearing, loss of reality, loss of life or property to any student suffered while participating in this course for any reason whatsoever, including ordinary negligence.

ENGLISH & LITERATURE

At Nafallen University, the English and Literature department draws upon works known and unknown from within and without the world. Students will acquire knowledge previously considered forbidden or otherwise verboten which they can then parlay into literary excursions of their own.

NAFALLEN UNIVERSITY

ENG 101: Freshman Literature
Prerequisites: Recommended concurrent course work in LAW 220.

Read core literary novels correctly sharing how to kill for pain, pleasure, and/or posterity. Read short stories and poetry that incorrectly describe killing, torture, and police procedures, and analyze how the story or moment could be improved through accuracy. Capstone project: create a literary work displaying accuracy regarding torture, killing, and evading detection on all levels. Extra credit awarded for students who successfully implement their story beyond the classroom walls.

ENG 103: Literature of the Other
Prerequisites: ENG 101 recommended.

Celebrate and dissect noted literary works created by the Other. Investigate serial killer autobiographies, gravedigger short stories, and an epistolary novel between a celebrated Satanist and his lovers among other works. Term paper will focus on exploring what Other authors contribute to the general knowledge base.

ENG 104: Creative Non-Fiction

Learn how to weave just enough fantastic into your true-life story to make it a bestseller. Practice creating sympathetic villains target audiences crave, and improve diction choices to make the audience feel their skin peeling back and life ebbing away. Master symbolism to take your life story to the next level. Take this course to turn your violence into profitable art.

ENG 155: Human Poetry for Outsiders and Non-majors

This course is an introduction to the complex and toothsome artform of human poetry. Students will gain experience explicating both classics from the old masters of poetry, as well as new works pushing the boundaries of the medium. Students will learn how the ordering of simple words can evoke some of the juiciest human thoughts and emotions.

ENG 232: The Genealogy of Blindness
Prerequisites: ENG 103, PHL 103, BIO 320.
Completion of and passing the campus eye exam is required.

Taking as its principal text Ernesto Sabato's *On Heroes and Tombs* (particularly the section titled "Report on the Blind"), this course maps the development of representations of blindness in literature, employing Sabato's novel as a hermeneutic. This course's exceptionally lengthy reading list is broken up by frequent "associative" lectures on the eye (as model for circular time, as sex object, as agent of malevolent omniscience, as representative of the nonhuman world-in-itself, etc.) which students with "sensitive" dispositions are encouraged to skip. The Genealogy of Blindness is the only accredited academic course in recorded history to openly address the threat that the Brotherhood of the Blind poses to the world of the seeing. Over the course of extended, strenuous, and often disorienting readings, students come to appreciate the illusory nature of the clinical division between "psychotic paranoia" and "normalcy," a distinction the blind mercilessly exploit for the furtherance of their malign purposes. Students, upon swearing to secrecy, are required to see this course to its fulfillment. The importance of physically attending this course's final exam, a group activity demonstrating the dialectic tension between enucleation and the Greek notion of katabasis, cannot be overstated.

ENG 269: Approaches to Joyce's Finnegans Wake
Prerequisites: ENG 101

Finnegans Wake has challenged readers since it was first published in the 1930's. Many are the mis-miss-mysteries contained withinwithout. Underwith the direction of celebated Joyce scholar Isav Kinn, students shall be awakened to the dark occult meaningings of Joyce's dreamprose. Simultaneous class readings of differant sectons will reveal the sinister underpiinings of Joyce's narrative as consonants war with vowels resulting in eldritch revelations garroteed to alight little pyres in the studeetudee fundaments. Homeoverk consisting excluesively of reading, re-reeding, and re-re-reedingwriting of cellickted passages shall alproduce insights misstical and blerghhhitjuntovularrrrrrrrrrkodeertobuttsentitiencelywoooooooooooonumb.

NAFALLEN UNIVERSITY

ENG 470: Bone Fiction
Prerequisites: BIO 250 "Bone Lab
Additional fees: One-time fee of $140 for an introductory bones kit

Tens of thousands of years before the written word, mankind was telling stories with bones. Join celebrated author and co-professor Chastize Kaine on an exploration of this most ancient and visceral form of fiction. Students will learn the history of bone stories while also composing their own works using materials both found and harvested. (Counts as a History credit towards the Forbidden Epochs specialization.)

FASHION

Through Fashion studies at Nafallen University, you'll be sure to turn heads clear around with the designs that make a difference. Countless eyes have popped and mouths fallen agape to never shut again as designs from graduates have been displayed on the runway ramps of New York City, Paris, London, and Tokyo. Make a fierce statement, and welcome to the Fashion department.

NAFALLEN UNIVERSITY

FAS 130—Intro to Funeral Attire

It's well known that the second-best part of death is the after party, and students interested in understanding the role of clothing in creating the perfect funeral atmosphere should take this course. Covers past, present, and future trends in funeral fashion for the living, dead, and anyone in between.

FAS 140—History of Executioner Garb

This course provides students with an overview of trends and experiments in executioners' clothing from prehistory to the present, including the best wardrobe choices for various common killing methods. This course involves several mandatory field trips.

FAS 141—Future of Executioner Garb
Prerequisites: FAS 140 required; prior applied ritual murder coursework recommended

Guided by the "dress for the job you want, not the job you have" principle, in this course students plot the exciting future of execution and ritual murder methods by designing outfits to suit them.

FAS 202—Abnormal Tailoring
Prerequisites: 100-level fashion coursework or permission of instructor

This course teaches the fundamentals of tailoring for non-human and extraterrestrial body types. Due to the wide variety of possible projects students can pursue in this course, it may be repeated for credit.

FAS 253—Comfortable in Your Own Skin
Prerequisites: FAS 202

Learn how to tailor and style a variety of skins in this hands-on course, which primarily focuses on custom garments made from a client's own species.

FAS 320—All Eyes on Me

This advanced course prepares students to style individuals with extraordinary quantities and placements of eyeballs. Covers TV, magazine, and boudoir shoots, and has an optional internship component (FAS 321) the following semester.

GENERAL SCIENCE

Science is your friend, for as far as it can take you. In our general science department, students can explore a diverse array of disciplines, from biology, to physics, to chemistry and beyond. Fire up your Bunsen burners, adjust your microscope, and embark on your studies in science!

NAFALLEN UNIVERSITY

SCI 100: Introduction to Unnatural Sciences (for non-science majors)

An introductory course that covers the basics of unnatural sciences: alchemic properties, aura reading, manipulation of dark matter, and ritualized magic. Students demonstrating exceptional aptitude in these areas may be considered for student government positions involving, among other activities, review and interviewing applicants for open faculty positions.

BIO 129: Introduction to Human Nutritional Sciences
Prerequisites: None

You are what you eat. In this introductory course, students will learn how what we eat makes us become what we are. As the class progresses, students will learn how various minerals and elements can affect change in the consumer, as well as the effects of consumption of human hair and flesh, and other chemicals both raw and cooked. Students with food allergies and other intolerances are encouraged to register.

BIO 250 Osteolaboratory "Bone Lab"
Prerequisites: SCI 101

Focused course on hunting, unearthing and identifying skeletal remains. This course includes lab work and field work off-campus and outside of normal class hours.

BIO 310: Principles for Decapitation

Students in this hands-on class will learn the basics of decapitation, including anatomy of the human neck and head. Learning the proper way to effectively remove heads from shoulders and which vertebrae is the crucial one to aim for while performing the art. Internal decapitation will also be touched upon although that's a bit trickier to accomplish without high-speed trajectory. The differences in swords versus axes and other weapons are covered in depth as well as the damages caused by each. The choice of weapon module is focused on helping the student learn which to use based on the desired result. Some targets deserve to be hacked rather than sliced cleanly and less painfully and this class is designed to allow the student to differentiate how to choose his or her weapon to make the most of their task. Once the basics of the act of decapitation are learned and tested theoretically, a lab is offered for an additional fee to allow the student to practice on cadavers before they move on to BIO: Decapitation 311 where live volunteers are recruited to help the student master the art of decapitation.

BIO 312: Night-Blooming Flowers

Learn about the history and mythology of night-blooming flowers as well as their power in rituals and spell work. Particular attention will be paid to poisonous night-blooming beauties including Datura, Nicotiana, and Cestrum, or Night Blooming Jessamine. Learn about proper dosage using live subjects. Attend just for the knowledge or pay an additional $120 fee to cultivate the poisonous plants for your home garden (leather gloves required). Note: This course meets at midnight.

BIO 320: Topics in Simulated Hypertrophy
Prerequisites: All course applicants must complete and sign the questionnaire appended to the department workbook, Beyond Good and Evil: Medical Ethics for a New Order.

This course focuses on cytological expansion, exploring its potentiality in a robust, cross-disciplinary environment thoroughly disentangled from cultural stigmas and taboos. Utilizing a diverse range of technology, from genetic manipulation to biological synthesis, students are encouraged to redefine the limits of cytology, exploring its potential impact over a spectrum of diverse fields of study. It is the purpose of this course to extract cytology from its confines in the pathology lab and to embrace the towering, cellular expanses that have every potential to redefine the relation between "life" in the particular and "Life" in the abstract. This course is highly recommended for students interested in cellular anatomy, since the dramatically truncated conceptual boundaries of typical cytology courses render intimate textile interaction with cellular material highly implausible. Mandatory Lab on Thursdays in the basement of the Polstere Admin building. HAZMAT suits are available from the Tome Dome Campus Bookstore in the closet adjacent to the "Dream Erotics" section.

BIO 321- Human Sustainability and Viability in the 21st Century (and Beyond)
Prerequisites: N/A

No.

BIO 380: The Fantastic Body of Kyle Russett
Prerequisites: Permission of the Science Faculty, class size limited to 9

One of the first graduates from Nafallen University, Mr. Kyle Russett of Crisp, TX has over the decades dedicated his body to the further education of Science students at Nafallen. The cohort selected by the Science faculty for the semester will receive Mr. Russett and perform the necessary rites and rituals to kill him. It is then their responsibility over the course of the semester to study Mr. Russett's corpse in excruciating detail, noting the ulcers, lesions, wens, scars, and other damage his body has taken, internally and externally, reanimating the corpse before the tolling of the semester bell. As is tradition, if the cohort fails in their task, they will serve as future semester material-however, Nafallen is proud to report a thus far unbroken streak of successful semesters. Will this mark the 309th time that Kyle Russett is returned to the land of the living, or will yours be the first cohort to fail?

BIO 388: Cirripedology/Biofouling Barnacles
Prerequisites: 200-300 Level BIO Courswork strongly recommended

This course teaches the genetic editing of barnacle DNA with the goal of mass sinking of ships and entire navies. These arthropods secrete a cement that is one of the most powerful natural glues known to science. Students will examine the process of strengthening this adhesive to prevent barnacle removal. Students will also study the potential for the genetic modification of the parasitic barnacle sacculina carcini, known to zombify crabs. The student will develop preliminary research questions with the goal of determining if barnacles with the proper genetic editing, could invade and take as a host, any human entering a body of water. The potential for an army of superspreading barnacle parasites taking over the seas will be investigated and a group research study conducted. Co-taught by Professors S. Snyder and C. Morgan.

BIO 414: Fear Responses in Higher Primates
Prerequisites: Conformation to DSM-VI definition of Paranoid Schizophrenia preferred.

See how they run. See how they run.

BIO 495: Disease Creation
Prerequisites: At least 12 credit hours of prior BIO courses.

As prior generations of geniuses created works of art like HIV, Lyme, and Covid-19, this course will challenge students to apply their knowledge to create new strains of existing diseases and their own unique diseases. The final exam will consist of students releasing their creations upon impoverished and vulnerable populations.

ENT 101: Nurturing Necrophila Americana

In this beginner entomology class, students will become familiar with beetles and then move to focus on the magnificent and best bug out there: the American Carrion Beetle, or Necrophila Americana. Understanding and appreciation of this beetle are but only a few of the lessons to be learned in this course. Students will learn how to properly care for and establish a thriving colony of this important member of the greater community common carrion beetle. These workhorses of the insect world revel in the dirtiest work of all: consuming decomposing flesh. At course completion, each student will have a small terrarium colony to take with them. Please note: students are prohibited from taking small mammals from anywhere on University grounds to feed their beetles. As the University cares for its own colonies throughout campus grounds, students must find food sources beyond the University boundaries for their beetles.

ENT 102: Flesh Devouring Beetles
Prerequisites: ENT 101

If students enjoyed ENT 101 and passed with a C or better, they are invited to take ENT 102. Flesh Devouring Beetles. This class builds on the knowledge established in its predecessor and introduces students to a variety of beetles in both the Silphinae and Nicrophorinae families of flesh-eating beetles. While these beetles mainly feed on wild animal carcasses, human remains are a treat. This class will introduce students to all 175 species members, including the rare and endangered American burying beetle. While it only exists now in four states, our University proudly cares for a thriving population in our woodlands. While observing these beetles burying a carcass, students just may learn a thing or two. By course completion, students should discover a beetle that perfectly suits their needs and general locale.

ZOO 231: Animal Summoning
Prerequisites: SCI 100

Talk to the animals! And they will listen! Through hands-on lab experiments, students will learn the words and rites to summon and command animals from the insect, reptile, and mammalian animal groups.

ZOO 232: Swarms
Prerequisites: ZOO 231 with a grade of C+ or above

(Continuation of ZOO 231: Animal Summoning) This course builds on previous knowledge of animal summoning to expand students' practicable abilities. Swarms are an integral part of animal-based intimidation, and despite their reputation, can be a safe and powerful tactic for new learners. In this semester course, students will learn to summon large numbers of animals for a singular purpose, such as destroying crops, causing panic, and spreading disease.

Core concepts: collective animal relationships, animal handling and safety, comprehension of abstract instructions to produce practical results. Animals will be provided. Companion animals will not be counted for a grade.

MED 103: Autosurgery

You are not a good surgeon until you can operate on yourself. In this course, students will learn to tolerate pain, as well as how to keep their hands steady even when heavily medicated. With proper training and equipment, students will be able to remove tumors from their own brains and perform a heart transplant on their own body. The course requires a lab fee. Applications should include next of kin to notify in the event of an unsuccessful final exam.

GEOGRAPHIC STUDIES

The globe we call Earth wearily spins towards oblivion. As we prepare for the Masters to return, it will be right and good to know where it is best for Them to return, and you will know those places, seen and unseen, as you embark on Geographic Studies here at Nafallen University. A faculty spanning this world brings an ocean of knowledge in which you will want to dive and drown in.

GEO 110—Cartography I
Prerequisites: None

Students in this course will study techniques of measuring and translating various geographies used throughout history. From ancient Mesopotamian methods, through to the Middle Ages and mapmakers such as Giuseppe "The Mad Mapmaker of Bologna" Enzione, to contemporary cartographers using esoteric methods such as psychic surveying and timemapping, students will be ready to explore the world in a new way.

GEO 160—Parasitic Twin Cities of The World
Prerequisites: None

As a way to foster a world-wide community and cultural exchange, major cities around the world have entered into familial relationships with cities from far and wide. But what of cities subsumed by their hungry, greedy twins? This survey of parasitic twin cities looks at the influence of these subsumed metropolises and how the cultural mycelium of these occulted cities influences the shape and design of the dominant and surrounding conurbation. Students will learn to identify where the boundaries between the parasitic twin cities lie, and how to gain egress without awakening denizens who may seek to prevent a resurgence of the lower city into our realm.

GEO 212—"Australia": Fact or Fiction?
Prerequisites: GEO 110

For nigh on many decades, tales of a land called "Australia" have propagated our news, schools, and culture. Since noted Dutch opium eater Willem Janszoon claimed in a feverish reverie to have discovered a land in the Pacific Ocean, a cabal of politicians, economists, and religious leaders have perpetuated the lie of this fanciful land, populated by clearly outlandish and imaginative animals born of deluded minds. The open-minded student will have the conspiracy exposed to the harsh light of truth-that there has never been nor ever will be such a thing as "Australia". After examining the evidence, the motivated student will also learn how to use that evidence to The Masters' advantage, using the (clearly fallacious) concept of "Australia" to eclipse those islands, waterways, and other land masses and areas that would be suitable for The Work without the public-at-large's prying, judging, stupid eyes.
Course taught by visiting professor and cartographic national treasure Dr. J. Wilburn

GEO 230—Transdimensional Territories I
Prerequisites: GEO 110 (MTH 151 Crowlean Geometry recommended)

You recall the days of grade school when you would gaze with wonder at the globe on your teacher's desk. Spinning it you would dream of traveling to perhaps Asia, or Europe. As you grew older, you looked down with disdain at those who espoused silly theories of a "flat" Earth. Well, buckle up buttercup, because your view of a 3-dimensional world is also woefully inadequate and backwards. In this exciting course, you will begin to understand that there are parts of this world that are mere projections of higher dimensional landscapes. Some are conveniently located near campus, and those with eyes and a supple, open mind can see them. Vistas that are impossible for ordinary people to perceive, let alone describe. You will see such beautiful, terrible sights, and you will never see our world the same way. Lab sessions at **THE WENDY'S ON MAIN** are required, students being responsible for arranging transportation to and from **THE WENDY'S ON MAIN**. Waiver to be signed prior to enrollment. In cases of spatial madness, we regret no refunds are permitted.

GEO 412: The Submerged City
Prerequisites: Enrollment in Archaeology Honors Program, Geography Studies Dept. Chair approval

Semester long field trip to Mustang Island to explore newly discovered structures below the waters in the Gulf of Mexico. Focus will cover 2 areas of current archaeological interest: The real-world application of underwater archaeological techniques, and the proper use of sacrifice as appeasement to the eldritch salt-water beings who dwell therein.

HUMANITIES

Laughable as it seems, given the inevitable conquest of our world by the Glorious Masters, Nafallen University offers a wide range of humanities studies with the goal of adding to the Masters' discipleship.

NAFALLEN UNIVERSITY

HIS 102: History of Violence
Prerequisites: None.?

Examine how individuals, small groups, governments, and corporations successfully apply violence to achieve their goals. This course examines the effective nature of both real and perceived violence to bring about worthwhile results. Students will be given local targets throughout the course and must demonstrate the best type of violence to obtain professor-assigned outcomes.

HIS 302: Exploring Ancient Torture Devices
Prerequisites: HIS 102 recommended.

Using ancient torture devices curated from around the world, this elective introduces students to torture from bygone days. Each week, visiting lecturers will introduce a favorite device, delve into its history and historical record, and demonstrate the device's potential. Students taking this course commit to finding an ancient torture device or recreating one to add to the University's collection. The term paper for this course centers on the defense of the most effective ancient torture device; A-level papers will include convincing visual aids. Alternatively, students may opt to put their woodworking and welding skills to use and modify an ancient torture device and demonstrate its new potential in lieu of a term paper with professor approval.

HIS 436: The History of Smells
Prerequisites: Olfactory-capable students only.

They drag you into a fast-food restaurant, cement memories in our mind, and are the sole reason why someone would exclaim in a crowded room: "OK, who the hell did that?" They are smells, and while you live with them daily, you probably aren't aware of their rich history. From neanderthal sweat to Henry VII's "secret lady sauce" to the honeytrap capabilities of dire wolf flatus, this class will examine the exciting history of smells and how they have evolved over the eons. Students will also partake in a lab element, where they will be required to introduce five unique smells to the class over the course of the semester.

HUM 101: Classic Languages

This course will focus on M'guthal, the "language" of the Masters, so that students may have a solid foundation for communicating with our Eldritch superiors. Students will quickly discover M'guthal is but a human categorization and "language" a human construct for the ways in which the Masters communicate their will to us. For some students, even one class session of this course will prove too much for their fragile minds to take in. But for the receptive student, the special student, a chord will be struck that achingly resonates in their soul, and they will be obsessed with learning all they are able to. A special seminar on M'guthal phonology presented by visiting professor Dr. Johannes Kayshu is sure to stir an all-consuming madness deep in the students' heart.

A special seminar on M'guthal phonology will be given by the esteemed lexicologist Dr. Whateley of Jakeshort University at the start of the semester. Arabic will also be covered, so students may better understand the nuances contained within the original text of the unabridged Necronomicon. The completion of this course is required before progressing onto Conjuring and Ritual Rites, and is recommended alongside Deep One Anthropology.

HUM 104: Deep One Anthropology
Prerequisites: None (However, HUM 101 is recommended prior to or during this course)

This course will encompass an in-depth look into the past, present and future of the Deep Ones. While the Deep Ones have often been regarded as a separate species from human beings, modern scholars have challenged this widely held belief. Once a month, field studies will be conducted in the historic town of Crisp, in which students can immerse themselves in the local culture and observe what has been coined the "Crisp Look" of the town's inhabitants firsthand. A visit to the city of Fg!Tiolp Y'ha-nthlei may also be in order pending meteorological conditions and permission from the Church of Depths.

HUM 221: Advanced Prehistoric Civilizations
Prerequisites: None.

This course will provide students with a foundation of knowledge on the most prominent pre-Atlantean cultures, such as the Hyperboreans, the Serpent People, and the inhabitants of Leng and Mu. Students will learn the origins of these species and cultures, the factors that contributed to their rise and fall, and the legacies they passed on to other civilizations. Students will also learn how the doom of these past peoples is mirrored in the decline of subsequent societies, including our own.

ARC 360: Artifact Discernment
Prerequisites: HIS 102 recommended but not required.

Is that an actual hand-stamped clay talisman from the reign of Nebuchadnezzar, or a mass-produced souvenir? Does that lead tablet inscribed with curses date from Roman Britain, or is it a 20th century forgery? Learn to tell the difference through the use of carbon dating and theoretical necromancy.

NAFALLEN UNIVERSITY

ART 388: Special Topics: Crop Circles

This 8-week course offers students insight into the finest crop circle-crafting techniques, while helping them avoid the pitfalls of beginners. Students will explore the origins of crop circles, learn how to best choose a canvas, and see crop circles for what they truly are and always have been: art. By the end of the course, students will be able to create an original crop circle of no less than 12 feet in diameter. Student limit of 12 per class, 2nd half of the course will take place on Koombs Family farm.

MAG 100 Magic: Essentials

From selecting the right tree from which to fashion your wand, to choosing the right material for your attire, Magic Essentials will ensure you are on the correct path for magical success. The semester is divided into three sections-the first is an intensive 3-week retreat where students will hone their meditative prowess under the guidance of Professor S. Robbins. After this retreat, students deemed suitably receptive will participate in a second three week intensive where they will collect and create the "tools of the trade" (wands, cloaks, chalk, etc.) while charging their nascent powers in the John Dee Memorial Stadium and Ritual House. The final third of coursework will see individual student performances including but not limited to true disappearing, summoning, and elemental creation/transmogrification. Prior to beginning the class, students will be required to sign a waiver under a full moon pledging fealty to the University, absolution of Nafallen University Faculty and Staff for any harm to the student's physical or mental health, and vouching for the utmost secrecy of all course materials under pains of expulsion from Nafallen University and other punishments as determined by the Council.

MAG 101: Magic Circles
Prerequisites MAG 100

Students will be given instruction in creation and use of magic circles to protect themselves from the emanations they summon. Specific attention will be given to both the inner and outer circles as well as the drawing of a five-pointed star. Faculty necromancers will instruct the class on the Cabbalistic signs of the Sepiroth, the Enochian language, the Book of Soyga, the Heptameron, and the Gran Grimoire. Faculty alchemists will demonstrate the proper use of silver cups, holy water, horseshoes, mandrake roots, rosaries, garlic, asafetida grass, salt, and mercury. The course will culminate in the ritual summoning of a demon by each student. Students are required to have life insurance and up to date emergency contact information.

MAG 102: Cursed Objects
Prerequisites MAG 100 and MAG 101

Building on the skills acquired in MAG 101, students will study the fine art of turning ordinary objects into items of misfortune bringing bad luck, dire illness, and even death to their owners. Any ordinary object can be imbued with demonic energy: mirrors, paintings, dolls, clothing, cars, tools, furniture, masks, cutlery, rabbit's foot, or coins. The goal of each student will be to curse an object of their choice belonging to someone else. Grades will be assigned on a sliding scale of ruin and death to the possessor.

RIT 224 Sacrificial Rituals

In this exciting course, students will study the various forms of ritual sacrifice performed through time immemorial, up to and including the present day. In addition to the practices, students will also learn which deities these rituals were intended to appease, and whether the sacrifice had the desired effect. Sacrificial rituals surveyed will include The Aztec *Xochiyáoyotl*, The Peruvian *Noche de Los Niños*, Celtic Esusian and Post-Esusian Rituals, Tibetal Tantric "Ecstatic" Sacrifice, and more.

RIT 319 & RIT 320: Procuring Men for Human Sacrifice
Prerequisites: This is a two-part course, taught in the Spring and the Fall. Students must sign up for both courses.

The first semester of Procuring Men for Human Sacrifice will introduce intermediate/advanced witches to the finer points of selecting appropriate tributes. Members of the class will learn practical misandry, the ins-and-outs of the sex offender registry, and advanced butchering techniques. Each student will be responsible for procuring the sacrifice for a single class session, but chalk, salt, blood, knives, and ritual tattooing supplies will be provided by the university. Students will be graded on their in-class participation and the quality of sacrifice(s).

For the second part of the course, students must also enroll in Introduction to Women's and Gender Studies (WGST 200) at Texas A&M,* as the class will focus on teaching students to pretend to be impressed by that one guy who took WGST 200 just to argue with everyone. Students will work together as a group for the final exam and should be aware that killing the target from WGST 200 early is understandable—but will result in a failing grade.

* Permission to enroll at Texas A&M is not needed; the instructor knows we will be there.

NAFALLEN UNIVERSITY

MUS 201: Mayhem and Music

This sophomore level music history course explores the best music for your passion. Discover your preferences between spiraling orchestral crescendos, deeply disturbing dirges, Viking death metal, and intricate mystical chanting among many others. Students will also study how sounds including crashing furniture, gunshots, power tools, moans, threats, and banshee-like screams can enhance music. To pass this course, students must demonstrate how their musical preference both disguises and enhances an act of their choosing.

LEGAL STUDIES

So much of what is necessary to enact the Will of the Masters unfortunately lands outside of the narrow and antiquated legal systems in place at all levels of society (local through to national). Nafallen University prides itself on having a one-of-a-kind slate of coursework dedicated to operating outside of those systems, discovering innovative loopholes in the legal labyrinth to ensure that the Will is manifested into Action.

NAFALLEN UNIVERSITY

LAW 105 Introduction to Law

Students embarking upon their education of the Law have no doubt had their minds polluted by depictions of the law in movies, television, and literature. Here at Nafallen University, the faculty of Legal Studies have made it their mission to disabuse students of these dangerous notions. Over the course of this semester long study, you will learn that the Law is no trifling conceptual construct to order human society, but a tangibly, terribly *REAL* entity who is very displeased, and who will mete out justice very soon. You will learn its name, contemplate its supposed paradoxes, and recognize its presence in the gaze of a murderer, the rantings of the lunatic, the leavings of the public defecator. You'll see what constitutes the most egregious of "crimes" against the beautiful face of Law, and beg to make it clean again. A portion of class time will be spent on site at the Crisp County Courthouse where students will be required to take class notes on the guilt and potential repercussions that litigants ought to face.

LAW 111: Hearsay and Heavy Metal
Prerequisites: None.

Survey course on history of the legal profession, beginning with British witch hunts (1550) through 1990's "Satanic Panic" in USA. Students are encouraged to question and/or defend the use of gossip and torture as valid legal instruments.

LAW 112: Exorcisms as Evictions
Prerequisites: LAW 105

In this semester, students will hone their debate skills as they argue the legality of exorcisms, addressing the questions: Does a priest/shaman/therapist have the legal right to evict a demon from the body of its host? Should there be recompense for any damage inflicted during the process? Should the homeless demon then become a ward of the State?

LAW 152: Ethical Sacrifices
Prerequisites: LAW 105 and PHL 103

When choosing source material for a ritual or procedure, it is critical to consider the legal and ethical implications of choosing such a source. In this course, we'll explore the history of sacrificing the innocent and challenge that notion by examining several key legal cases in this arena to prepare students to think critically about where, how, and from whom they are acquiring bones, blood, and other organic material. This course encourages open discussion of all viewpoints and thus will culminate in a debate titled, "The Baby or The Bastard?"

LAW 201: Tu'runthigal Law

An introductory course in Tu'runthigal Law. Judicial history and evolution, covering the original star-quarried tablets YUOIRMKD brought to primigenius Earth, the codices of Bx and Lethmor, the approved appendices from the Text of Tisbälberg, and other foundational documents.

LAW 202: Eldritch Case Law
Prerequisites: LAW 201

This masterclass will be delivered by four prestigious visiting professors. Each class will be an in-depth analysis of a seminal legal case from Eldritch jurisprudence, in which the instructor was involved either as judge, prosecutor, defense lawyer, and/or defendant.
Week 1-2: Crisp v. United States (civil rights)
Week 3-4: State of Massachusetts v. Prelmeth & Sons (manslaughter, destruction of property)
Week 5-6: Asmo'Goriath v. Johannsen (maritime hit-and-run)
Week 7-8: Akeley v. Di-Let-Rab Inc. (identity theft)

LAW 220: Forensic Evasion I—Beginning Topics
Prerequisites: LAW 105, ENG 101 recommended.

This course will introduce students to the myriad means by which they can thwart forensic investigation by notorious criminal/investigator Prof. Mikhail Enodet. Classes in the traditional analysis of crime scenes and evidence will provide a solid basis of knowledge which will then be applied in lab settings. Working in teams of two, labs will consist of a "criminal" committing crimes ranging from the mundane to the violent, and an "investigator" who will seek to collect enough evidence to warrant arrest. Crafty "criminals" may wish to throw "investigators" off the trail by combining different evidentiary modes (e.g. documents and blood splatter, missile trajectory and DNA residue, etc.) Do not fret, students will switch roles halfway through the semester. Unsolved cases from the semester will be collected in the Enodet Register, one of the necessary texts for the course (re-published each calendar year). Extra credit given for those who can solve cases logged in the Register.

NAFALLEN UNIVERSITY

LAW 420: Forensic Evasion II—Advanced Topics
Prerequisites: B or Higher Final Score in LAW 220 and Entry in Enodet Register

This second course on Forensic Evasion, also led by Professor Enodet, notorious and as yet unconvicted criminal/investigator, will see students focusing exclusively on the Enodet Register and the "criminal" cases within. Students will be encouraged to find real-life applications for the crimes detailed, as well as ways by which they may further obfuscate efforts to solve them. Obfuscation may be both natural and supernatural as per the students' other skills and education. As a capstone project, a suitable "patsy" will be selected from the Crisp, TX area whom the crime can be pinned upon, and the "crime" then executed under the direction (but not direct involvement) of the nefariously clever Prof. Enodet. Note: waivers exonerating Nafallen University or its faculty of any wrongdoing must be signed, notarized, and filed prior to Day 1 of classes.

MATHEMATICS

We are delighted that you are considering a program of Mathematics here at Nafallen University. Many students have passed through our corridors and gone on to great notoriety applying the various theories they first learned of here. Our faculty will help you discover and exceed your potential, in service to our ancient Masters. With slide rule, abacus, and hard work, you will surely be rewarded with unimaginable knowledge. We look forward to solving for the unknown variable with you.

MTH 107: Basic Geometry for Summoning Majors
Prerequisites: None

This course will teach students the basic geometric components of summoning circles and other ritual shapes. Students may be asked to provide their own compasses, rulers, and sacrificial objects.

MTH 141 : Irrational Al-Jabra I
Prerequisites: None

Students in this introductory course will learn about variables seen and unseen, known and unknown, and the equations advanced Al-Jabraists have attempted to solve for millennia.

MTH 151: Crowlean Geometry
Prerequisites: None

Study the shapes of 2, 3, and 5 dimensions as discovered by occultist Aleister Crowley.

MTH 161: Essentials of Enochian Squares
Prerequisites: None, but waiver to be signed. Recommended MTH 141 previous or concurrent

In this course, students will learn basic theories of Enochian angel communication via so-called "Magick Squares". In addition to lectures, there will also be a practicum to be performed under the canopy of night in the John Dee Memorial Stadium and Ritual House.

MTH 201: Dark Logic
Prerequisites: Evaluation by faculty

Some things just don't seem to make sense, do they? Ah but they do, and MTH 201 will instruct you as to what real "sense" is. The average human mind, untrained in the concepts you will learn in Dark Logic, would boggle and revolt at the concepts you will learn about in this 6-week intensive course. Prior to class, prospective students will be evaluated and "tuned" as appropriate to ensure maximum receptivity to the coursework therein.

MTH 222: Pythagorean Number Theory
Prerequisites: MTH 141 and 151 suggested

Revel in the esoteric wonders of numbers real and unreal suggested by the Cult of Pythagorists.

MTH 247: Pre-Sumerian Counting Rituals
Prerequisites: MTH 141

Students taking MTH 247 will journey into pre-Sumerian times, using materials thought long lost, from Dr. Dunnsany's private collection. By the end of the 12-week course, you will become an expert in non-decimal base number systems, and be able to flawlessly perform rituals of worship at the John Dee Memorial Stadium and Ritual House.

MTH 261: Advanced Concepts of Enochian Squares
Prerequisites: MTH 151, MTH 161, and astral recommendation from at least 1 Enochian entity

Students will become familiar with Enochian Square concepts that would startle even the clever mind of John Dee. Students will apply concepts of MTH 151 to circumscribe new shapes and contact new, more complex entities. Students will gladly spend the majority of the class and personal time ensconced in rigorous study in the lower level of the Ritual House.

MTH 321 Heremetic Calculus

Advanced mathematical students will delight in awe at this exclusive offering from Nafallen University. Thought lost to time, the Mathematics department some years ago came into possession of scrolls dating from the second century CE which were determined to be an authentic branch of Mathematics pre-dating so-called traditional Calculus by at least 1500 years. These concepts were set down by "The Mad Greek" Polsipopulous who history tells us was expelled from the Pythagorian Cult for being too radical. Polsipopulous travelled along the Northern Nile, accumulating knowledge which he then synthesized into the corpus of study we call Hermetic Calculus. Among the many sundry concepts students will learn of: Rhombal Division, The Set of Midnight, Imaginary Integrals, Indeterminate Forms in Time, and many others. By the conclusion of the course, students will begin to comprehend the meta-numerical rules truly undergirding this plane of existence, and nonsensical manmade systems of Mathematics that have held sway for far too long.

MTH 334: The Geometry of Labyrinths
Prerequisites: MTH 321

In addition to providing a quick overview of the labyrinth in literature by way of readings from Virgil, Ovid, Chaucer, and Dante, this course focuses on the highly artificial geometrical environment particular to labyrinths. Game theory, cryptography, and "calculus of deception" (a little-known mathematical system with applications unique to this course) all coincide to provide a robust and tantalizing grasp of the labyrinthine as it relates to both physical architecture and subjective interior spaces alike. Of particular focus is the "multivalence" of the labyrinth, or its simultaneous role as a space and "non-space." This course is divided into two sections. The first half of the semester is dedicated to the strenuous mathematical study of the labyrinth's duplicitous nature. It is during this period that students are encouraged to remain in constant contact with the campus behavioral health unit. By the semester's second half, students are expected to have "transcended" the labyrinth, an academic shift entailed in the transposition from mathematics to the "poetics of geometry." This phase also entails the obtainment of the highly esteemed "Mark of Icarus," readily identifiable in students by the radiance of their facial features and their corresponding inability to focus their gaze on objects close at hand. Since this class meets in the infamous "Infinity Mirror" room (Wilson Classroom Center 304), students suffering from spectrophobia are strongly discouraged from enrolling.

MTH 351: Applied Gemantria
Prerequisites: MTH 261, approval of faculty

You have now attained knowledge of the angels and demons, beyond those suggested by Solomon and the honorable Dr. Dee. You have accessed and communicated with these entities via Enochian Squares, Riemann Spheres, and Crowlean Hypercubes. Now take the next step to shapes we cannot speak of in this catalog, that will control those entities and direct them to act upon our dimension in accordance with their Masters. With our Masters. All hail our Masters.

MTH 361: Unreal Analysis
Prerequisites: Permission of instructor and at least 90% in MTH 201

A further study of concepts first learned in MTH 201. Students will be expected to provide rigorous proofs of the obscure nature of things. Students will be provided with bound journals of flesh to set down their findings in their blood. Failing students will provide the journals for subsequent semesters.

MTH 442: Differential Topology Concepts
Prerequisites: MTH 351 and EGR 181, and permission of instructor

As our advanced students make way for our Masters, it is good and right that we should build for them grand structures that welcome them and reflect their terrible majesty. Our world is so uncomfortable for them though, which is why in Differential Topology Concepts, you will learn of the shapes that will please them and allow them to remake the world in their way. When the world is washed away, take pride that your sacrifice was for their greater glory. All hail out Masters.

MTH 499: The Final Digit of Pi
Prerequisites: MTH 361 and permission of the department head

Traditional mathematicians believe that there are numbers that never end and stretch on to infinity. But you know better-you know there is an end. You have studied long and hard for this course, and you will reach that end. When the final digit is set down, it will signal to the Masters that we are ready. Ready for what? That would be telling, and the Masters are doing the telling. All hail our Masters.

MTH 4#1: Unrealized Mathematics
Prerequisites: MTH 361 and PSY 101

This course will expand upon the concepts of advanced mathematics while completely disregarding the fundamentals of the field. Not only will students learn how to construct equations in alternate realties, but also to actualize those theoretical models in their own space/time. Students will learn how to cope with most of the known results of their counterfactual actualizations. The final project will be the development of an alternate mathematical system that must work in and maintain an actualized pocket dimension.

OCCULT LIBRARY SCIENCE

A special offering of Nafallen university, the Occult Library Science program is world renowned for its program of preservation and dissemination of rare and occult tracts and manuscripts. Students successfully completing this certificate program are ensured an esteemed spot in any of their choice of libraries hidden away in the nooks and crannies of this world.

NAFALLEN UNIVERSITY

LIB 101: Introduction to Occult Texts

Students will be introduced to cataloguing and provenancing rare, frequently forbidden, and often dangerous printed books, manuscript tomes, and scrolls (both vellum and papyri). By learning basic palaeography, students will be able to assign broad dates to those manuscripts written using the Latin alphabet. They will also learn the principles behind assigning anonymous MSS to possible authors by comparing them to signed examples. Additional instruction will be provided on how to identify and describe any marginalia, bloodstains, runes, evil eyes, or any other kind of mark. Assessment will be by exam (60%) and by continuous assessment (40%). In the latter case, students will be assigned selected MSS and printed volumes to catalog and provenance.

LIB 201: Wards and Magical Reading

Students will learn how to detect magical wards that protect occult books and manuscripts, which can be fatal to the careless. By using magical spells and, occasionally, optical and digital technology, students will develop techniques in detecting wards and allocating percentile scores to each scroll or volume according to the Deadly Decimal System of classification. They will also learn to use spells to safely remove wards and to read obscure calligraphy, typefaces, and languages. Assessment includes an oral exam (40%) on their knowledge of spellcasting (students must learn the spells by rote). Improperly recited spells can have drastic consequences for the student, or (worse!) the warded object, or even the Edgar K. Howell Memorial Library itself! Students will also be examined (60%) on accurately assessing the degree to which scrolls or tomes are warded and to remove any wards they detect. The wards concerned will be largely harmless, but one or two items will bear lethal protections, so students must take extra care in the presence of these occult works at all times. All students are required to sign a disclaimer absolving Nafaullen University and its personnel from any responsibility for death or injuries sustained due to unsatisfactory spellcasting.

LIB 301: Occult Scribes and Texts

This course offers a broad overview of some of the leading scribes of occult works and their texts, from the anonymous ancient Egyptian Book of the Dead, through the medieval Necronomicon (of which we have selected transcripts made by Dr Mortimer before his disappearance) and Heinrich Kramer's 16th-century Malleus Malleficorum, to some of the more obscure and otherwise unknown MS notes and treatises by such modern scholars and practitioners of the Dark Arts as 19th-century wizard Johann Georg Hohman, Marie Laveau (the Voodoo Queen), and Aleister Crowley, as well as the archival records of occult experiments conducted by the Third Reich. Assessment is by exam (60%) and a written assignment (40%) on an occult scribe or text chosen by agreement between the student and faculty.

LIB 310: Haunted Books and Manuscripts

In the course of a long career, occult librarians occasionally have to deal with books and manuscripts that are haunted by a ghost. Typically, the ghost will be the spirit or animus of a once-living person who was personally associated with the book or manuscript concerned. In many cases, this person wrote the inscribed text and such ghosts are of particular interest as they can sometimes speak with the living and provide useful information about the book or manuscript's origins and purpose. They might also be able to elaborate on difficult passages within the text. The course will focus on the techniques used in identifying haunted books and manuscripts, establishing the nature of the spirits that haunt them, and in communicating with ghosts. Five haunted books from the Perford Occult Collections in the Nafallen University Edgar K. Howell Memorial Library's basement will be made available for study. Students will be assessed on a single group project (100% of the assessment) to be submitted before the completion of the course. They will need to identify and communicate with the ghosts concerned so that they may learn more about the books and their contents.

LIB 401: Conservation of Occult Books

The conservation of ancient and recent occult manuscripts and books is an important but painstaking process. Some books and scrolls are unique and therefore irreplaceable, requiring particular care in their conservation. Students will learn about book-binding, repairing vellum and paper documents, restoring book covers, and retouching faded or stained text and illuminations. They will also learn about the materials used to make manuscripts and books. These include animal/human skin to make vellum or to wrap a book's wooden boards, animal or human gut used for binding, and the types of ink used (mineral compounds, plant dyes, animal/human blood). These materials often lend magical power to grimoires or to the wards that protect the books and MSS. The material often has a close relationship with the author of the text (e.g. could the author's own blood have been used for the ink?). Students will each have the opportunity to carry out supervised conservation of ten less important books and manuscripts over the academic year. Assessment will be continuous (100%) on this practical work for the duration of this course.

LIB 410: Possessed Books and Manuscripts

A demonically possessed document is very dangerous to handle directly as the demon will try to influence or possess anybody coming into physical contact with it. While demons can be identified and communicated with, they cannot be trusted to answer any question truthfully, and they will always try to manipulate a reader in some way. No single person is therefore permitted to read a possessed book or communicate with the demon on their own. Students will work in a team to identify the demon and the text as well as to determine why the demon possessed it. Students will be assessed for their individual contribution towards a group project (100%). Each student will take notes during weekly communications with the demon and will compare them to establish the consistency of the demon's speech. All students will receive charms, wards, or potions to protect them from the demon, but they must provide their own blood to make these magical protections. Also, students will sign a disclaimer absolving Nafullen University and its personnel from any responsibility for death or injuries they sustain from failing to conduct themselves with due care while interrogating a demon-possessed document.

PHARMACEUTICAL SCIENCE

We bid you welcome to a special series of courses offered by our austere Nafallen University. Over our decades of study in the wilds of South America, we have brought back formulae and concepts you will not find in any other North American university. The basic courses set a solid foundation upon which you will explore strange and wonderful corners of the pharmaceutical universe which culminate in a final practicum semester interning with the pharmacy staff at Crisp Memorial Hospital. We wish you the best and look forward to administering your medicines.

PHM 130: History of Medicine I
Prerequisites: None

An introductory course in the history of medicine in various countries. Medicine to cure, medicine to harm. What makes something a medicine? What can medicine not cure? How can medicine be used to prolong life, and to snuff it out? Some of these answers await you.

PHM 240 Powders of South America
Prerequisites: AGR 261

Professor Wyppthorpe brings some of her special knowledge to this course in the various powders found in South American countries. Learn of the *yerga*, which can paralyze the most hearty of men, or the *usotad*, which can be used as a hypnotic. *Xaldupo, kudaro*, and the revelatory *swioplatan* will also be administered and studied. Upon completion of the course, those students who have survived the pop quizzes and exams will be considered as candidates for advanced coursework in the Pharmacy Science program.

PHM 250 Mind Dehancement Via Pharmaceutical Administration
Prerequisites: Passing score and survival of PHM 240

You've seen your weaker cohort succumb to the *Xaldupo*, and after your *swioplatan* mind-journey, you understand the difference between dehancement and debilitation. We will study more, oh so much more, about how the pharmaceutical sciences can aid in the coming of Those We Serve in The Dark. We will titrate amounts to show where that thin line between mind plasticity and mind warping lies. Glory be to our Masters.

PHM 260: Mantis Extract Methods I
Prerequisites: Survival of PHM 250

In this course, we start a study of how *swioplatan* is produced in its most natural form. The course is theoretical in nature, though by now, you'll want to taste and taste again the sweet and slightly bitter preparation to keep your mind in that pleasant, plastic, dehanced state.

PHM 270 History of Medicine II
Prerequisites: Acceptance of application to the Pharmaceutical Science Certification

Students will further study a hidden history of medicine, and how medicine can help us discern what the cure really is, and what the illness really is. Lab sessions will be held in Tymothee Forest Preserve.

PHM 300 Binders—An Overview
Prerequisites: Passing score from PHM 270

Through your study of the various pharmaceuticals in previous coursework, you have learned that it is impossible to administer these medications on their own without detection-the bitter tang gives them away and is revolting to the palate. In PHM 300, you will learn about a variety of agents which can be bound to these drugs which mask the tell-tale signs of the active ingredient. By the end of the course, students can expect to have created forms for the Medications of our Masters which are indistinguishable from common over-the-counter medications, and may be easy to replace in the local pharmacies.

PHM 320: Studies in Administrations
Prerequisites: Passing score in PHM 300

It is one thing to partake of the Medications of our Masters yourself, but the larger goal is for the community to become dehanced, pliable, and compliant to the will of our Masters. To that end, Studies in Administrations will provide an overview of the various means by which medicine can be administered. Which medicines are more effectively administered via aerosol versus in pill form? Which medicines are more potent administered sublingually versus an IV drip? The student will be expected to become facile in all routes of administration.

PHM 360: Mantis Extract Methods II
Prerequisites PHM 260

The *swioplatan* is now something you must partake of regularly. The soothing song of the Mantis your soundtrack to this life of yours. In PHM 360, students will directly commune with the glorious Mantis and recognize its esteemed place in the true Order of things. Successful completion of the course will depend on commensurate fealty shown to our Dictyopterian Cohort along with demonstrations of proper extraction methods not just from the Mantis without, but the Mantis within.

PHM 400: Practicum—Internship at Crisp Hospital
Prerequisites: Passing score in PHM 320 and acceptance into Intern program at Crisp Hospital

Armed with the knowledge you have attained throughout the program, now is the time to put it into action. Students interning at Crisp Hospital will work alongside professionals in the Pharmacy preparing medications and administering them to the appropriate patients. You'll recognize some of them from your lower-level courses, the ones who didn't pass but have not "passed (away) out of the program". Some may even surprise with their value to the greater program as hosts for medication, or sustenance for the Mantis. In either case, you will administer the medications most suitable for the variety of patients as well as more widespread administrations to the non-hospitalized populations of the surrounding area.

PHILOSOPHY

Whether they were rulers in Ancient times, or cranky professors in the ivory towers of academia, humans have thought about the big ideas across the millennia. Knowledge, Truth, Right and Wrong—these are but some of the base concepts of Philosophy. At Nafallen University, you'll learn the Unknowable, the Truth behind the Truth, and that Right and Wrong are flawed concepts having very little to do with what matters.

PHL 103: Introduction to Natural Philosophy
Prerequisites: None

This introduction to the philosophical nature of the natural and physical universe assists students in understanding the relationship between human beings and the observable and unobservable universe in which they live. This course will help establish working definitions of a systematic study of nature, including a working knowledge of humors, magicks, alchemic principles, cosmological physics, and important teleological principles.

PHL 144: Educational Philosophy 1: Publick Education Grades 0-12
Prerequisites: None

Those pursuing teaching certification for publick school children will find this course on Educational Philosophy most enlightening. We'll be studying seminal texts on Educational Philosophy such as "Spoil the Teacher" by D. Baker and "Tract on What to Teach, 3rd Ed." by Ehlke & Hopkin. Innovative field studies will be held at Crisp Publick Schools, where Nafallen students can watch the light drain from the local children's eyes as they are sorted and placed into their appropriate post-Publick education tracks.

PHL 224: Applied Natural Philosophy
Prerequisites: PHL 103, PHL 224-L Lab corequisite

In Applied Natural Philosophy, students will continue their study of subjects included in Introduction to Natural Philosophy with the addition of practical applications for various units of study. Students will be required to:
- extract, store, and balance the four humors of the body, as well as understand the practical implications for the imbalance of humors;
- cause change to occur in conformity with Will using with applied magicks
- extract, craft, store, collect, and dispense various alchemical sundries
- track the movement of celestial objects for purposes of ritual
- prepare sacrificial material for the summoning of minor daemons and other spirits (actual sacrificial ritual will not be covered in this course)

PHL 244: Educational Philosophy 2: Collegiate Education
Prerequisites: PHL 144, evaluation by Philosophy Faculty

A very special course indeed, for here the secrets undergirding collegiate education are revealed to those worthy of the knowledge. Students who pass the rigorous application process for entry will learn the true purposes of collegiate education, and how the coursework, the housing, the dining, and the *buildings and grounds themselves*, work in conjunction to create the panic, fear, *ennui*, jealousy, rage, and more that are all a part of the modern collegiate educational experience. Learn the techniques that are utilized to make the most important sounding coursework for a program of study the least effective and useful. Discover the ways in which faculty can minimize their actual delivery of useful information in favor of lengthy flights of boring monologuing. Upon passing the course, students will be sworn to secrecy as to all they have learned.

PHL 290: Shadows of Self
Prerequisites: PHL 103 recommended

In this class, students will explore the idea of the "shadow-self", defined by F.R. Guisson as "the self that does the dark things our public self would not". Students will first summon and contain their shadow self, then proceed to debate them in classroom lab sessions on points of ethics such as autonomy, justice, and so forth. Passing scores will be awarded for students who come to see that their shadow-selves are the correct ones.

PHL 310: Nihilism I
Prerequisites: A feeling that nothing you're doing really matters

This initial offering in Nihilism serves as a reminder and a basis for the idea that nothing you are doing right now really matters. Students will embark on a systematic approach to breaking every course, relationship, and affiliation down to its essential, empty essence. The capstone activity will consist of a presentation with the theme "It is all for Naught".

PHL 403: Ethics of Ritual and Summoning
Prerequisites: PHL 224 (Student must also be in good academic standing)

Ethics of Ritual and Summoning focuses on the ethical questions pertaining to the enactment of ritual summons and other forms of dangerous magicks. A range of real-world ethical problems and their theoretical explorations will be covered, including:
- Original sin and its consequences
- The Eldritch gods and nihilism
- "The Whole or the Part": what to sacrifice and why
- Legal and ethical distinctions between sacrifice and murder
- Famous contemplations on the greater good and the lesser evil

Included in the class is a senior writing requirement explaining the basic ethical assumptions made for their senior practicums. This course is a standard co-requirement for most majors in applied magicks and ritualistic studies.

PHL 410: Nihilism II
Prerequisites: Demonstration of sufficient detachment from all material things

Taking PHL 310 as its base, and extending it to and beyond its rational conclusion, students accepted into PHL 410 will further break down every waking and sleeping activity to the gaping maw of Null which gnashes and rends behind the veil of existence. In the face of this realization, weaker students may decide to end it all, whereas the most suitable of students will discover their purpose for the Masters, and set about it with grim apathy and resignation. Students will "pass" the course when they fade from existence into oblivion.

POLITICAL SCIENCE

Thank you for your interest in the Political Science department here at Nafallen University. We have worked since the University's inception to create a program of study which will educate the dedicated student in the ways of the political world. We have seen nations rise and fall over our lifetimes, but political systems underlying this cycle continue to persist. Our historical courses offer a look at the past to see what ought to be recovered and revived, and what mistakes leaders have made that we will not repeat. Students advancing through the degree program will also learn about ways to work with those in political power to ensure that the true Power's goals are being implemented and worked towards. We look forward to seeing your studious faces in our classrooms and lecture halls, ready to embark on making a difference in the world.

NAFALLEN UNIVERSITY

POL 130: Hollow Earth Geopolitics—An Introduction
Prerequisites: None

In this introductory course, students will gain perspective and knowledge of those political forces that act unseen upon and within the nations of men. The farce of political parties around the world will be revealed through seminal texts by Beauregard, Viani, and Hayes as students become familiar with Teedian society. Students expecting to advance in their political science studies must successfully complete this course.

POL 146: Eastern European Political Movements of the 1600's
Prerequisites: None

A survey of the lesser-known systems of political power and theory from Eastern Europe in the early to mid-17th century. Before the acquisition of territories by Russian and Polish forces, a unique hybrid of power structures terrestrial and extra-terrestrial found fecund expression. A key element of study is the *Podziemni zjadacze grzybów*, and its regional variants in and around modern-day Poland. A final project by students will be a paper and presentation on connections between *Podziemni zjadacze grzybów* and contemporary political philosophies.

POL 161: Siberian Political Systems 200-1000
Prerequisites: None.

Offered once annually by Professor Yousey. In remote areas of the Taiga, a political ideology came to rule significant portions of the Siberian Steppe prior to the Hun invasions. A precursor to what would come to be known in Eastern Europe as *Podziemni zjadacze grzybów*, this ideology represents in some ways a more true (some might say, brutal) view of who are truly the Masters of our world, and what we owe to Them for our existence on this plane. A select cohort of students will be selected based on completed assignments to volunteer time with the state congressional district's office.

POL 181: Subaquatic Politics
Prerequisites: POL 130

Far beneath the depths of the oceans, systems of power and its application undreamt of by even the most capable of terrestrial political science await you. Here you will become exposed to Brachyurean concepts which will speak Truth to Power and deafen those who cling to traditional forms of government. Labs will be held at the Michael A. Cavagnaro Aquarium and Oceanic Research Facility where students exhibiting acceptable allegiance will be introduced to Crustacean Envoys who will provide further instruction and guidance.

POL 220: Interdimensional Political Science
Prerequisites: POL 146 and POL 161

Up to this point, students will have become familiar with the systems of political thought more closely aligned with the Masters. But these systems are but mere shadows on the wall compared to what the true elements of political play are for our Masters in and beyond the world. Students in POL 220 will become more familiar with these true elements, and how we can implement these concepts within current political frameworks, and what emerging political systems hew closer to the ideologies that really matter.

POL 230: Rhetorical Attack Methodologies
Prerequisites: POL 181 and POL 220

Throughout the course, students will read treatises on how to attack opponents of Correct Political Ideology using rhetorical methods. In continued lab time with the Crustacean Faculty at the Michael A.Cavagnaro Aquarium and Oceanic Research Facility, students will discover the words and phrases that will both mentally and physically cripple their nemesis in political debate. High performing students will be encouraged to further their studies in advanced Political Science—low performing students will be summarily prohibited from further study in the program and will serve a different purpose in the times to come.

POL 320: On The Turning Away—A Blind Eye Approach
Prerequisites: Successful completion of POL 230

Much like the royal Fungi, some political concepts grow best in the dark, limited in exposure to current governmental entities. Using concepts from POL 230 and direction from the Crustacean and Teedian Faculty, students will begin the work of transition from terrestrial political interests to a cosmic ideology more in keeping with our Masters, while employing subtlety and occult methods to hide our work from prying, interfering eyes. Students are expected to demonstrate successful implementation of policies that are banal on the surface but will have longer term implications to our Masters' benefit.

POL 400: Advanced Concepts in Hollow Earth Geopolitics
Prerequisites: Permission of faculty after application review.

Your tongue forms the consonants of change, and your voice clacks and clicks in sounds that can move others to your will-their Will. An idea is becoming a movement, the movement of hordes of shells making a rhythm of war—but is it a war when so many have willingly sacrificed themselves towards the Masters' greater designs? Fighting is the most futile of exercises in the coming dawn. The small cohort of students making up the POL 400 class know this all too well. Your mind is now not only receptive but driven by a political mania to do what it takes to ensure Teedian and Crustacean interests are represented in the halls of our towns, our states, and our country. All hail our conquering Masters.

PROGNOSTICS

We know who you are.
We know you are going to join our student body, and that you will take up studies in our program.
We know how it will end. We will not tell you.

PGS 101—World History of Prognostication
Prerequisites: None

In this course, students will study prophetic texts from various points in history and from a variety of cultures. Students will be encouraged to determine which were true acts of predictive talent, and which were the acts of charlatans looking to exploit their audiences. The final project will involve a student profile of a selected seer.

PGS 141—Prophetic Artistry
Prerequisites: PGS 101, Signed Waiver

Not all fortunes are communicated via the written word-indeed, art is sometimes a more effective medium to communicate about things to come. The Department's collection of rare but startlingly accurate prophetic art dating from the early current era through present day will be the basis of study. It is not uncommon for students to become obsessed with certain pieces, hence the necessity for a signed waiver absolving the University and Faculty of any wrongdoing in the case of unhealthy preoccupation or madness that results from exposure to these grand pieces. Successful completion of the course will be critical for acceptance into the Prognostic Certification Program.

PGS 161—Hydromancy Methods I
Note all PGS classes above PGS 141 require admission and good standing academic position in the Prognostic Certification Program
Prerequisites: PGS 101, PGS 141 and Acceptance into Prognostic Certification Program.

A creek, a river, a lake. Perhaps you have traveled over the ocean by aeroplane, and peered down seeing more than water below you. Maybe even in your own bath room, in a sink full of shaving foam and warm water, floating there, a terrible scene you can't help but feel is about to happen-but who will believe you? The right audience will. In this first course of the PCP program proper, you will learn to recognize the images that reveal themselves to those with the eyes to see. Course time will be split between lecture and lab study at various natural water settings around Crisp.

PGS 222—Aruspex Studies
Prerequisites: Acceptance into Prognostic Certification Program

Effective methods of haruspicy, and the types of fortunes foretold by the type of animal used will be reviewed. Copious lab assignments will see student dive their hands deep into the fetid entrails of fowl, fish, rodent, horse, racists, and more, while reporting upon the sights, smells, and sounds revealed to them of things to come. A capstone project will be accomplished with materials provided by Khilljoy Memorial Home.

PGS 250—Automatic Auguring
Prerequisites: Acceptance into Prognostic Certification Program

Some of the most effective practitioners of the fortune telling arts are those who have no recollection of the methods by which they attained their information. These austere augurs have unwittingly become channels for messages from our Masters that slip through the cracks of time to tell of us times to come. Among the activities discussed and performed in class will be abolishment of the ego via meditative and medicative methods, interpretation of signs and symbols, and recognition of portentous clues in all aspects of waking and sleeping life.

PGS 300—Advanced Concepts in Prognostication
Prerequisites: Successful completion of PCP coursework at the 200 level

The gibbering you used to take for nonsense is now telling you so much. You are compelled by some extra-terrestrial force to scribble these missives down for all to read and benefit from. But beneath that chatter lies even more subtle glosses, accents, and other sub-language elements which tell a grander story. The Masters want you to hear them until your ears bleed, and then they will show you the sights they want you to see, until your eyes cry out their vitreous gel. And then They'll use your tongue and throat to speak.

PGS 400—Practicum in Prophecy
Prerequisites: PGS 300 survival, and acceptance by PGS faculty

Students will remove the following page from the course catalog, and smear it with the feces, urine, blood, kidneys, intestines, and brains of a suitable mammal sacrifice no smaller than a field shrew, which will then reveal the final project title, materials, timeline, and theme to the student for presentation and approval by the PGS faculty. You will already know whether or not it is accepted. Upon successful project completion, students will be directed to inter any and all records of their project work in the Nafallen University Library Catacombs. Unsuccessful completion of the project will result in "mob justice" at the hands of faculty staff and the student body, including but not limited to; tarring and feathering, drawing and quartering, and leng t'che.

PSYCHOLOGY

It is through understanding and control of the human mind that the Masters will find no resistance to their dominance over this plain. We welcome you to the offerings of the Psychology slate of courses, and look forward to shaping your malleable and pitiful minds to the eldritch Will of the Masters.

NAFALLEN UNIVERSITY

PSY 101: Introduction to Psychology
Prerequisites: None

In this introductory course, students will begin to pull back the pink, fleshly layers of the mind, revealing the pathetic human impulses and diseases which make the species bound for ultimate cosmic failure, except as preparers of the way for the glorious Masters to reign supreme.

PSY 133: Mind Control I-Introduction
Prerequisites: None

In this introductory course, students will gain an understanding of the most effective methods for elementary mind-control. You will learn tried-and-true Neuro-Linguistic Programming elements to plant the seed of your Will in the fecund field of the mind, to grow into Action. A final project involving class demonstration will separate the Adept from the Pliable.

PSY 209: Inflicting Pain
Prerequisites: PSY 101

Torture has been a useful tool for everything from weapons of war, treatments of the mentally dysfunctional, and resolving marital disputes. Properly inflicting pain, however, is more than the brutish application of fists, nails, and torches. True pain requires mental games as will be taught by this course. A discount for this course is available to students who provide subjects for classes.

PSY 212: Applications in Psychology I
Prerequisites: PSY 101

Students taking PSY 212 will practice the lessons learned in PSY 101 in real-life situations. Through ad copy reads over the campus radio station and cryptic entries posted to Olde Wyathscope's Quarterly Concern, watch in wonder as your words elicit such sinister deeds in your campus community and wider.

PSY 233: Mind Control II: Advanced Techniques for Brainwashing
Prerequisites: Passing score of "Adept" in PSY 133

Students determined to be "Adept" in PSY 133 (Mind Control I-Introduction) are encouraged to further their study of Mind Control techniques in this advanced course. Here, students will take on the role of "Daddy/Mommy" who will break down "Pliables" to weak and empty vessels, ready to please at all cost, no matter what the ask. Students will also learn effective ways to shield their minds from external human control, and ways to fake "pliability" to act as agents of subterfuge against those enemies of the Masters.

PSY 301: How to Fake Feelings
Prerequisites: Required course for all enrolled sociopaths; an elective class for everyone else.

Students will learn how to create convincing feelings in one-on-one, small, and large social interactions. Need to convince someone you love them? Hate them? Need to show remorse for hitting Fido? Need to convince others you're grieving? This class is for you. The instructor will cover the basics of emotional reactions and delve into how to coordinate body language to coincide with believable emotions. The professor will recruit locals to test student mastery in a variety of situations. Students need to master at least five emotions to successfully pass the class from the following list: anger, sadness, grief, love, lust, joy, disgust, fear, uncertainty, contempt, surprise.

PSY 345: Orthodox Psychology
Prerequisites: Enrollment subject to psychological screening.

This course details the disorders of the conforming mind, such as a willingness to enslave oneself to society's expectations and prohibiting the exploration of the full self beyond what is deemed "normal." Students learn how to navigate conversations with individuals suffering from orthodox psychological conditions and conduct research relevant to their areas of interest.

PSY 363: Torture with Common Household Objects
Prerequisites: PSY 209

Metal kitchen whisks are great for creating peaks in egg whites, but did you know they can also be heated up and used to whip/brand a confession out of someone? A rack is certainly handy when you are trying to weed out infidels, but did you know four Roombas and a strong ball of twine will also do the job? Not everyone has the money or space for an iron maiden, waterboarding table, or a shin bone crusher, but so long as you have a box of 12 penny nails, a pressure washer with a Depends undergarment, and a meat tenderizer, you should be able to torture just fine. This class will teach students the tips and tricks for inflicting pain with simple items available in most households.

PSY 402: Sleep Disturbance Creation.
Prerequisites: High score on SAT (Sadism Aptitude Test) and permission of instructor.

In this advanced course, students will learn how to cause sleep disturbances, such as sleepwalking, narcolepsy, and traumatic nightmares using brain stimulation of the cortex and amygdala. Includes additional lab instruction in techniques of administering psychoactive drugs to create psychosis and suicidal impulses in reluctant subjects.

RELIGIOUS STUDIES

It is often quipped that in polite company, one does not discuss matters of taxes, death, or religion. In the Religious Studies department at Nafallen University, we certainly do talk about religion, for it is through Religious Studies that we find a means of control and of preparation for Things to Come. You will find through our coursework a window into the many facets and forms that deities take, none of them a quite complete picture of the scale and scope of the Masters, who direct and control us all in thoughts, words, and deeds. We look forward to inviting you into our temple and pulling back the curtain behind the altar.

REL 101: Paganism
Prerequisites: None

Paganism has always existed, the term was first used in the fourth century, coined to gather together all those who were not of Christian, or Jewish faith. All things were "Pagan." If Paganism is simply not belonging to an Abrahamic faith, how may we make a calculated and scholarly study of the "Pagan faith?"
During this year long course, we will be practicing tantric meditation and non-Euclidean time manipulation in order to study every deity and every numinous being to have ever meddled in human affairs enough to be worshiped.

As this is a freshman course, we offer Yith-Assisted anti-aging, as an alternative for students who have not yet mastered combating the ravages of time.

REL 102: Theosophy
Prerequisites: None

Taught by Kuthumi, this course is less a scholarly exploration of Theosophy and more a guided meditation of chelaship. Students will be expected to enter class ready to forgo the pleasures of the flesh and meditate upon the true power of the spiritual self. Though guided practice students will engage in both the creation and emotional manipulation of thought-forms, as well as engage in the use of faith as a means of superiority towards lesser enlightened individuals.

REL 108: Studies in Cult Recruitment
Prerequisites: None*
*To clarify: Having no prior experience with this topic is the requirement.

What is a cult? Why create a cult? Who joins a cult? When will the entropic flame of this universe reach the end of its cosmic wick, leaving all that is transient and light to sputter into nihility? Where will you be when the gossamer pall that serves as the fabric of space-time is ripped asunder, reality torn to shreds by the non-Euclidian limbs and eldritch not-claws of ASH'MOGORATH FATHER OF THE SUNLESS DEPTHS. Whose name will feature in your mucus-sodden hymns as the holy dark descends upon eternity? These questions and more will be discussed over the duration of this semester-long seminar, as this course is most definitely a class, and not itself a cult in disguise.

REL 138: Mythical and Mystical Entities of the Jewish Faith
Prerequisites: None

Taught by the Dean of Religious studies, this course will discuss how the Jewish Diaspora adopted and disseminated its folklore in a way that helped pave the path for global mythology and an intertwining of belief. Students will study through texts and participatory dissection the similarities between sheydim, fae, demons, and goblins.

Students will be expected to learn and distinguish between various malevolent spirits, dybbukim, alukha'ot as well as understand the different between acceptable and treif magical practices.

REL 303: Heretical Exorcisms of the Middle Ages
Prerequisites: None but LAW 112 recommended

This course explores the overlooked history of exorcisms as they were performed by heretical movements between the years 1200 and 1500. Compiling rare source material attributed to diverse sects such as The Brethren of the Free Spirit and early European movements generally accepted as forerunners of the Order of Dagon, this course operates upon the well-founded assumption that readings in heretical exorcism accounts present a unique opportunity to study the phenomenon of demonic possession from a perspective untainted by the hegemonic narrative of Ecclesiastical authorities.

A secondary thesis, which has arisen over the years following the inception of this course, entails the study of the physics of possession. Given the anomalous operation of physical phenomena (or, in the discourse of this highly specific field of interest, "malphysics") that exclusively characterize cases of demonic possession in accounts disentangled from the metaphysics of the Christian Church, the "physics of possession," its causes, deterrents, and cosmic implications, are all quickly becoming central concerns for Heretical Exorcisms. As such, undefined and unannounced "clinical hours" may occur, which entail extended travel and overnight stays for the purpose of "case studies."

As paradoxical as it may seem, a working knowledge of "The Roman Ritual" is now highly encouraged for prospective students.

REL 322: Theriomorphism in Practice
Prerequisites: REL 101

This 3-credit course introduces students to the ritual practices and cosmological implications of worshipping prominent animal-headed deities. By semester's end, students will variously be expected to have encountered, gazed in marveling awe or melded themselves in unison with deities such as Anubis, Baphomet, and Narasimha.

REL 345: Living Religion—The Thuggee
Prerequisites: REL 108 recommended but not required.

This course focuses on the enduring and secret traditions of the Kali-worshipping cult known as the Thuggees. While formerly thought to have gone extinct in early Modern West Bengal, the class will experience the first-hand revival of their cultic practices. By semester's end, students will be expected to have familiarized themselves with mystical tantric intercourse, advanced human sacrificial techniques, and the wild dance of the blood-thirsty mother goddess herself.

REL 403: The Abramelin in Theory and Practice
Prerequisites: Senior Standing

This Senior level course will examine the various translations of the Abramelin as well as show the fallacies in the Thelema translation, discuss the history of the book, and prepare students for successful completion of the ritual so that they might summon their own Eldritch Guide.

REL 666: Comparative Satanic Studies: Theistic vs Atheistic
Prerequisites: REL 101

Satanism in all forms has existed far longer than the character it takes its modern name from. There have always been those who seek to please a dark master, who are urged to take the left-hand path of the id and slaughter in service to their own unpalatable wanton desires. There have also always been those who reject all masters, who seek pure freedom not only for themselves but for all of human kind.

One group is easily swayed to the mechanisms of the true occultist, a tool in an arsenal to be unleashed when theatrics are required. The other can be troublesome; how does one control those who rail against control?

In this course we will discuss the very nature of these faiths and study the religious ceremonies of both groups, with the ultimate goal of infiltration, manipulation, and digestion.

REL 777: Numerology and Angels
Prerequisites: 100-200 level Mathematics coursework recommended

Why 777? Why 666? Why do any numbers matter when math and numbers are false things created by man to explain an unexplainable nonsense world filled to the brim with lies? Angels, true angels, masses of eyes and flames and mouths exist not to serve man, but to continue the long lie of reality.

It is through the experience of mathematics that one may be able to unravel the conspiracy of angelic beings. Through use of numbers and formulae one may discern numinous beings and then force them to tell the truth about jet fuel melting the original John Lennon!

Students will be expected to make use of their own name and the names, social security numbers, phone numbers, birth dates, and other numerical information of their families to both confront the divine as well as steal identities to pay for any damages called by aforementioned divine beings.

REL 042: Everything
Prerequisites: A basic grasp of life and the universe

In 1978, author Douglas Adams made a joke in his radio comedy show, that the answer to life, the universe, and everything was 42. The joke was purposeful, mathematical, and cryptic. Those who discover the answer discuss the possible meaning in light hearted fun.

But this is no laughing matter. All things may be summed up into the number 42. This seeming innocuous number can be seen over and over again by those who are in tune with the universe.

Through this course and its associated lab, students will study not only the mysterious number and all of its strange permutations, but work to weaponize and take advantage of what the secret knowledge may grant in terms of power and knowledge.

COMMUNITY OFFERINGS: SENIOR STUDIES

This recent, exciting addition to Nafallen University's programming represents the connections we have made in our community as our influence grows. Specially tailored for life-long learners, and harvesting the expertise of those in the Crisp, TX area, we look forward to sharing knowledge that you just won't find anywhere else!

NAFALLEN UNIVERSITY

SS 100—Dark Crochet
Materials provided by instructor.

Alisson Fernays will teach you the dark art of crochet. This is not the crochet you learned at your grandmother's feet as a youth. No, this crochet will please acolytes of the Master, and perhaps even a Master themselves. Using materials such as twine, suture thread, tanned flesh, sweetbreads, and other esoteric and rare materials, by the end of the 6 week course you will be presenting tableaus that tell tales, labyrinthine narratives spanning eons of suffering and madness.
Monday evenings 7PM

SS 120—Quilting for The Masters
Material list provided prior to first class-experience with sewing and ability to lift 50 lbs comfortably recommended.

Twin sisters Deborah and Elisabeth Hogan have been avid quilters for over 5 decades. You have seen their tapestries showing the history of Crisp at the Centenial Commemoration, but they have more wonderful sights to show you. Join the Hogan Sisters for an exciting adventure in quilting, where your blood, sweat, and tears will be rewarded with the knowledge that you are contributing to the greater dissemination of the Masters' will. Class size is strictly limited to 12.
Wednesday afternoons 1PM

SS 140—Concerning Burial
Ability to move up to 100 lbs via barrow required
A unique combination of fitness class and lecture, Bruce O'Vale of Khilljoy Memorial Home leads this vital session comprising an overview of burial techniques from around the world. Students will learn pre-burial rituals to prepare the corpse for acceptable burial, what treatments to use in the soil to better utilize the deceased's natural chemicals, and best times for burial to feed the ever-hungry entities. Fortunately, at Nafallen, we are never in lack of bodies to practice burial techniques on, and we value the contributions of SS 140 students who are doing their part to set the table for the Feast.
Tuesdays and Thursdays 2AM

SS 160—Fun With Grimoires!
Knowledge of Zhou Mandarin, and Early Cyrillic preferred but not required, NDA signed in blood required.

If you consider yourself a reader, this is the course for you! University Librarian Farah Smith opens her secret library to SS 210 students (limited to 6 per 6 week session), where you will investigate (among others) such varied works as **PLATUE OF MURR** (The Sacred Guide to Cosmic Hegemony, ~BCE 1800), Астрономические знаки и знамения (Astronomical Signs and Portents, ~CE 150) , and a tome we cannot put in writing here, so forbidden and terrible is its name that it might blast apart the sanity of those who read it in this catalog.
Saturdays 1PM

SS 180—Estate Planning
Applicants with terminal diseases encouraged to apply

As the old expression says, "You Can't Take it With You", and with that adage in mind, Crisp Credit Union Lead Teller Taryn Bross will teach you the ins and outs of Estate Planning-critically, how to manage your affairs for the maximum benefit of the University, and for our Masters. You have worked so hard to amass your wealth, now ensure that it is put to good use for future generations of acolytes and servants of our Glorious and Terrible Masters.
Wednesdays 3PM

SS 200—Elder Sport
Physical examination by University Health Center staff required

Get up and move! This twice weekly course of activity is led by Mr. James "Big Jim" Wolthropp of Crisp Senior High School, and is designed to get your blood flowing. Each session will involve basic instruction in the sport of the day, then 40 minutes of game activity. Winners will be required to transport Losers to the Khilljoy Memorial Home after imbibing the necessary "spoils". Men and Women are welcome to participate after undergoing a thorough exam for "fitness" by Nafallen University Health Center staff. Let the Games begin in honor of our benevolent Masters!
Tuesdays and Thursdays after the Local News

NAFALLEN UNIVERSITY

SS 220—Senior Choir

Music makes the world go round
And we shall add our awe-full sound.
To make our Masters glad and haste
An end to our worldly waste.
Mme. Gertrude La'Fleur will on the harpsichord pluck
As the voices click and clack and cluck.
Hymns to Them you'll gladly learn
Even as you feel your mind begin to burn.
Apply now, no musical knowledge we require
To sing praise to our Masters upon the Grand Funeral Pyre.
Sundays at the Tymothee Forest Preserve 7AM

STUDENT LIFE

WELCOME FRESHMAN STUDENTS TO NAFALLEN UNIVERSITY!
ARE YOU A CRAB OR A MANTIS?
FIND OUT DURING THE FRESHMAN JUBILEE!!
THURSDAY AUGUST 20 ON THE COMMON AS THE SUN SETS ON THE HORIZON.
COME ONE, COME ALL, COME AS YOU ARE!
REFRESHMENTS PROVIDED BY THE CAFETERIA DEPARTMENT!

Representatives of The Crab Hive, The Mantis House, The League of NULL, and other fraternal houses will have tables and demonstrations to entice and enchant you. Music provided by the Nafallen University Marching Band (NUMB) will lull you into a daze from which you won't want to wake. Outside alcohol STRICTLY FORBIDDEN—our collegiate libation (The Fegan Trifle) developed by the Khemistry Klub will suit you just fine-bet you can't drink just one (and bet you can't drink more than three!) A fun time will be had by all and will barely be remembered the next day but for the curious marks inscribed just above your elbow-worry not!-these are but sigils of your fealty to our Great Masters and the educational adventure you are embarking on at Nafallen University.

Attendance fee included in your freshman tuition, other classes may attend for a sliding scale fee based on class standing.

THE TOME DOME

Your source for books, shirts, paraphernalia, and more!

At the Tome Dome, you'll be able to find all of the texts required for your semester! Many of the books required for classes are hard to find, and in fact, are expressly forbidden for sale in several jurisdictions and over the internet. The Tome Dome is the best place to find these obscure texts! You'll find the best* prices for your textbooks in our store!

Show your school spirit with shirts, hats, and sweatshirts emblazoned with the school sigil!

JUST IN: Nafallen Chalices! Drink deep all of your intoxicating libations from these nifty vessels!

The Tome Dome accepts all major credit cards, cash, blood, souls, and offspring.

*No guarantee is offered that these are the "best" prices. No exchanges or refunds given for incorrect purchases.

NAFALLEN UNIVERSITY SPEAKER SERIES

Each semester, Nafallen University invites a world-renowned speaker to the university for a series of talks on subjects of interest to the student body. This semester, Nafallen is delighted to welcome, from Harkendott University, Norway, Dr. Janet Petersen. Dr. Petersen is no stranger to Nafallen University, being one of the original faculty members in the Political Science department. She holds a doctorate in Political Science from Guison University in France, and currently teaches Political Philosophy from Harkendott University in Norway, and wrote the seminal text "Politics: A Critical Review" published by Maximillan Brothers (currently in its 19th edition).

The topic for her lecture series this semester, "The Scattering of Power-A Means to an End", promises to be an exciting overview of the ways in which anarchic chaos can help to eradicate current global power structures in the interest of fomenting an ascendant control paradigm by hollow-earth denizens. Students enrolled in the Political Science degree program may attend all lectures for free. The first and second talks will be open to the public for a fee of $5. The third and fourth of the series will be for Political Science students and Faculty only. Refreshments served after all sessions, with a meet and greet with Dr. Petersen after the first talk, where she will be happy to sign copies of "Politics: A Critical Review" purchased from the Tome Dome. No photography or recording allowed.

HOMECOMING

CHEER! CHEER! CHEER!!!

REIGNING STATE CHAMPIONS, YOUR NAFALLEN UNIVERSITY CANTANKEROUS CEPHALOPODS START THEIR SEASON NEXT TUESDAY AGAINST TEXAS A&M UNDER THE LIGHTS OF JOHN DEE MEMORIAL STADIUM!!

Blow your vuvuzelas, loud and proud, as the Ladies and Gentleman Cephalopods eviscerate the competition and clamber to the top of the pile!

The first 500 attendees will receive a "Charles the Cantankerous Cephalopod" lanyard!

Refreshments courtesy of the Cafeteria Department and Khilljoy Memorial Home!

Fireworks and Post-Game Flesh-Feast! WOW!

Half-Time Performance by the NUMB (Nafallen University Marching Band)

Contact Coach Bernard to volunteer at the game selling tickets, concessions, and cleaning up the effluvia and gore from the field!

FEE SCHEDULE:

The following lists of fees are intended as a guide. Nafallen University encourages students to secure funding via the Crisp branch of Upland Central Bank. We recommend speaking with loan officer Mr. Theodore Yulkson, a graduate of Nafallen University's business program, about a loan package that will suit your (and our Masters') needs.

All per semester unless otherwise noted:

Tuition:
$1,000 per credit up to 9 credits
$800 per credit for up to 18 credits
(Therefore, a full course load of 18 credits will be $9000+$7200 = $13,200.00 tuition + 15% handling fee = $15,180.00)

Bursar Fee
$500 payable in cash only—$20s and $5s only, securely wrapped in plastic wrap, in a plain brown paper bag, left under the trashcan outside the East entrance of the Tome Dome.

Bookstore Fee
$1,000 fee—this fee allows students access to the Tome Dome bookstore.

Student Life Fee
$2,000 fee—this fee goes toward Freshman Jubilee costs, one medium Nafallen University t-shirt, and campus beautification projects as needed.

Maintenance Fee
$3,000 fee—Fee going towards building and grounds maintenance.

Health Fee
$2,000 fee—Staffing and testing costs of student health center (additional fee assessed if students seek care at the health center)

Transportation Fee
$750 fee—Staffing and maintenance of faculty transportation in and around campus. No students allowed.

Cafeteria Fee
$1,000 fee—Staffing and maintenance of cafeteria facilities, plus one meal per week for students.

Dormitory Fee
$3,000 fee—Upkeep, maintenance, and staffing of student housing in and around campus.
An additional fee of $1,500 for a two-bedroom shared dormitory.

Inquiry Fee
$200 per inquiry—to be paid by Money Order made out to Nafallen University accompanying each inquiry submitted to the university.

FACULTY

Alexander Nachaj—Post-Graduate Fellow in Ritual Biology
Dr. Alexander Nachaj holds a Master's Degree in metaphysical anthropology and a Doctorate Degree in practical thaumaturgy. His ongoing research involves ethnographic fieldwork among the valley tantrics. In his spare time, he enjoys sojourning through the liminal realms and spending time with his cat. You can keep tabs on his whereabouts by visiting www.anachaj.ca. (*REL 322, REL 345*)

Anna Ojinnaka—Librarian at Nafallen University
After graduating with a first-class degree in R'lyehian Language from Miskatonic University, Anna decided to pursue a career in archaeology by working as an excavator on the Exham Prior Estate. Alas, such work proved quite maddening, and she found herself back at university working as a librarian instead. She's much more comfortable amongst books than ancient crypts. You can find her work in Love Letters to Poe, The Ghastling, and Ahoy Comics. (*EGR 210, HUM 101, HUM 104*)

Ben Arzate—Adjunct Professor
Ben Arzate received his Doctorate Degree in oneirology from Monk City University. When not teaching classes or chewing on human bones while naked in the campus quad of Nafallen, he has affairs with other professor's wives, hoping to get a National Book Award winning novel out of it. His published research, mad ramblings, and unheeded cries for help can be read at dripdropdripdropdripdrop.blogspot.com. (*BIO 495, COM 405, BUS 381, EGR 385, PSY 209*)

Carlton Herzog, Professor Nafallen University.
Professor Herzog attained his Doctorate Degree in Anarchist Studies by murdering the real Carlton Herzog and stealing his identity. His books include Murder Should be Legal, Evil is in the Eye of the Beholder, The Joy of Malicious Intent, and All that Hell Allows. When not teaching or writing, he can be found egging Proud Boys and Oath Keepers, pouring LSD into the Gatorade at Republican rallies, and impersonating the Devil at Pentecostal churches. Currently, he is on the FBI's Most Wanted List. His writing can be found at amazon.com/author/carltonherzog. (*MAG 101, MAG 102*)

NAFALLEN UNIVERSITY

Christopher Muscato is a distinguished lecturer, Covert Benandanti Fellowship Scholar, and recipient of the National Unheritage Trust Endowment for the Slow March to Nothingness. His trailblazing text on the blazing of trails as means of creating summoning circles in the pre-modern prairie has been called "Auashhhgsdhugbkhb" and "flmlfmlfmlfmlxrcks" by the Society of Undead Leaureates. Professor Muscato can be reached via astral projections or in his normal office hours at Nafallen University, occurring daily at the intersection of eternity and never. *(MTH 107)*

Cormack Baldwin—Professor of Animal Pseudoscience
Cormack Baldwin achieved his Master's Degree in the mud and the fear of the forest, and later his PhD in the deep salt sea. His research interests include animal magnetism (here meaning the magnets within animals), post-human knowledge, and increasing his power through harnessing the vastness of life. Along with his research credits, he is the life and death science archivist at Archive of the Odd. His laboratory can be found at cmbaldwin.carrd.co. *(ZOO 232)*

Prof. Greg Fewer, B.A., M.A.—Keeper of Occult Collections
Prof. Fewer graduated with a B.A. in Archaeology and Ancient Languages from Oxford University, in England, before going on to complete an M.A. in librarianship at Miskatonic University. His thesis focused on the university's collection of Sumero-Akkadian cuneiform tablets pertaining to human sacrifice among the ancient Sumerians and Akkadians. He was subsequently appointed to a two-year Fellowship in the Study of Ancient Texts at the library of Miskatonic University, during which time he updated and annotated Dr Cyrus Llanfer's "The Sorcerer's Apprentice", a typescript catalog of arcane texts housed in that library's Special Collections. Before coming to Nafallen University, where he was initially appointed Assistant Librarian, he served as an advisor to the United States Army about antiquities in Iraq (2006-2008). He continues to advise the United States government in a similar capacity. His most recent publication is "The Scholarly Career of Dr William Mortimer and His Strange Disappearance", in Arcane Research Letters, lii(2), 2019. *(Occult Librarianship)*

Dr. Henry Herz earned his Baccalaureate Degree (magna cum laude) in Criminal Justice, masters in Military Science, and doctorate in Xenomorph Anatomy, all from Miskatonic University. He conducts research on the effectiveness of experimental weaponry against exotic bioforms, as well as how to make chewing gum flavor last longer. Dr. Herz enjoys midnight walks in graveyards, surprise autopsies, and the smell of formaldehyde in the morning. Learn more at www.henryherz.com *(LAW 220)*

Miguel Fliguer is Distinguished Professor in Eldritch Culinary Sciences. His seminal book, Cooking With Lovecraft, is a classic of the genre and required reading for several curricula. He also sits in the Carter Chair of Acausal Temporal Paradox, every odd-numbered Tuesday, Thursday, and Sunday. The remainder of the time, Esteemed Visiting Entity Mi'Ke Slater pilots his human host from the year 7,004,645,221 BCE. in pursuit of knowledge relating to modern feloids of the interstitial skein. He is the author of the Necronomnomnom and Lovecraft Cocktails grimoires. Interested students need only visit the Amazon or seek an audience at RedDukeGames.com for supplemental materials. *(LAW 201, LAW 202)*

Hillary Lyon—Department Chair, Creative Writing
Professor Lyon will be teaching only two courses this academic year: Flowers for Emily: Poetry as Necromancy, and Through a Multi-Faceted Eye: Odes to Beelzebub. She co-authored (with Warren Flammenwerfer) two studies, I'm Too Sexy for My Cloak (on the curious phenomenon of warlock strippers) and The Glorious Glitter Hack (on the over-use of witches' glamours by members of the fashion industry). Her Neophyte's Handbook for Hiking the Mountains of Madness is required reading for all incoming students. She was granted tenure before any of you were born. *(ARC 360, GEO 412, LAW 111, LAW 112)*

Jennifer Shneiderman is an adjunct marine biology professor focusing her research on zombie crabs and their parasitic masters. She spends her free time humming Frank Sinatra tunes and decorating coffins with periwinkle shells. Follow her on twitter at https://twitter.com/jennifershneid3. *(BIO 388)*

Jeremy Billingsley—Professor Emeritus, Nafallen University
Dr. Billingsley earned his BA in Communication from Miskatonic, then transferred to the Lovecraftian Institute of Massachusetts (LIM) to earn his MA and PhD in spiritual communication and conjuring. He has published five articles for the Necronomicon Quarterly and has served as Midpriest for both the Hermetic Order of the Golden Dawn and the Order of the Dragon. In his free time, he enjoys communing with his long-lost childhood goldfish. You can find him on Twitter and his novel at www.sleyhouse.com. *(COM 102, COM 202, COM 326, COM 433, REL 403)*

John Kiste—Associate Professor at Nafallen University
Mr. Kiste briefly studied Agricultural Business Management at Yale University (until the well-documented BSE herd derangement of '99). He received a special Master's Degree at Miskatonic University upon presentation of his thesis, Proof of Possession in Prickles of Porcupines, and How to Familiarize Them for Occult Purposes. He won the 2006 Midsommar Award for Most Fractalated Crop Circle. You can find him at johnkiste.wordpress.com *(AGR 179)*

Jolie Toomajan—Professor of English and Gender Studies
Mlle. Toomajan received a Ph.D. in English from Ingolstadt University; her dissertation examined the

practical applications of vagina dentata as articulated by early twentieth-century women writers. She holds dual positions at Nafallen University in the Literature and Gender Studies departments. In her free time, she maintains Nafallen's whisper network and is auditioning to join the Empusa for fun. You can find out whether she succeeded by following @JolieToomajan on Twitter. *(RIT 319 & RIT 320)*

Joshua Bartolome—Professor of Goetic Computer Programming
After being expelled from Athabasca University's computer science department for allegedly using a dead student's hippocampus as a C++ compiler, Joshua Bartolome continued his studies in Nafallen University and received his Goetic programming graduate degree in 2016. Currently, he writes horrid and obscene short stories as a hobby. His most recent work, "Juramentado", will be published by Flame Tree Press in their upcoming Asian Ghost Stories anthology. *(CSC 101, CSC 116)*

Ms. Haynes, an oxygen-consuming flesh husk just like you, earned a Master of Dimensions at Nafallen University, where she spawned centuries ago. In her free time, she enjoys communing with aliens, frolicking in the poison fields, and plunging into the icy depths of the blood lake to find the only bit of warmth she'll ever know. You can find her if you say the magic words into your mirror or carve her name with a griffin's talon. (A harpy's talon also works but will take a respectable 10-12 business days to yield results, of course.) *(ART 388, LAW 152, PSY 345, SCI 100)*

M. Regan—Assistant Professor of Esoteric Floriology
Mx. Regan joined the faculty of Nafallen University in 2021, after overworked staff in the Environmental Sciences Department exhumed their corpse from the campus forest, filled their bones with a bioluminescent marrow alchemized from cursed soil, and set them to the task of grading papers. When they are not teaching, researching, or longing to return to the earth, Mx. Regan can be found gazing into the void, lemon balm growing wild in their hair. If you are looking for an extension on your thesis, please contact them on Facebook or Twitter @MReganFiction. " *(AGR 222, REL 108)*

Samir Knego—Visiting Professor, Fashion
Mr. Knego earned an MFA in experimental needlework by defeating its prior owner with his wits and approximately fourteen feet of off-black linen. Known for unusual perforation techniques and work that bridges fashion and anatomy, his designs have appeared in many nightmares and final moments. You can find his less sinister artwork on instagram @SamirKnego. *(Fashion)*

Anatomy Professor **Sherry F. Chancellor** received her Bachelor's degree in biology and went on to Avalon University in Tintagel for a Master's Degree in Medieval weaponry and completed an internship in proper usage of poleaxes, maces, broadswords and trebuchet. Upon completion of the internship, she graduated with honors from the Burke and Hare medical school. In her spare time, professor Chancellor enjoys teaching wolves and leopards to sing in harmony—her favorite song to hear them sing is Kumbaya. She also enjoys riding rhinos nightly when the moon is dark. Connect with the professor at SherryFowlerChancellor.com *(BIO 310)*

Tobin Elliott—Professor of Bioanthroarcheology, Nafallen University
Professor Elliott was found lost and wandering between the strange angles of an ancient ruin. He would only ask, ""Did you walk here, or take a lunch?"" His parents were never found, but it set him on a lifelong quest to continue their studies. When not examining some strange archeology, Professor Elliott volunteers at a Home for Wayward Flat-Earthers, or can be found adding to his work on defining the universe and providing three examples. You can find him railing at real and imagined injustices on his Twitter account, Tobin Elliott—Horror Guy" *(EGR 181)*

Trevor Childers—Associate Professor
Trevor Childers' doctorate in quantum chirology appeared in his hands upon waking from a strange, half-remembered dream that still haunts him to this day. After years spent walking aimlessly, he arrived in Texas to mold young minds and also teach. Outside of work, he collects mundane rocks and studies their effect on extraordinary rocks. *(HUM 221, MTH 431)*

Justin Burnett—Professor of Thrall Production and Maintenance
Justin A. Burnett is the author of The Puppet King and Other Atonements, to be published by Trepidatio Publishing in 2022. He's also the Executive Editor of Silent Motorist Media, a weird fiction publisher responsible for the creation of the anthologies Mannequin: Tales of Wood Made Flesh, which was named best multi-author anthology of 2019 by Rue Morgue magazine, The Nightside Codex, and Hymns of Abomination, a tribute to the work of Matthew M. Bartlett. His quarterly chapbook, Mysterium Tremendum, explores the intersection between horror and the holy. He currently lives in Austin, Texas, with his partner and children. *(BIO 320, ENG 232, MTH 334, REL 303)*

Larina Warnock—Professor of Lycanthropic Studies
Doc Nock holds a doctorate in Entrepreneurial Execution and is a silent partner in an undisclosed number of innovative, underground corporations that may or may not be operating illegally in the United States and beyond. In her spare time, she enjoys plotting economic catastrophes and howling with werewolves. You can learn more about her above-the-line activities at www.larinawarnock.net *(BUS 101, BUS 121, BUS 123, BUS 161)*

Persephone Potts(Lorraine Schein)—Professor of Ethical and Unethical Cannibalism
Persephone Potts has a PhD in Nocturnal Emissions from De Sade University and graduated with an MD in Electrocution summa cum laude from Con Ed Tech. In her spare time, she enjoys removing the tongues of street mimes, chloroforming her family and deleting Oxford commas. Her cooking show competition involving small dogs, deep frying and tempeh is currently in development. Visit her website at yrwrstnightmare.com or contact her at ppotts@psychopath.net *(PSY 402)*

R. Wayne Gray—Adjunct Professor of History and Practical Home Economics
On lone from the New England College of Metaphysical Design, Professor R. Wayne Gray teaches a variety of subjects ranging from alternative history to unique domestic applications. His recent book, The Complete Mold Cookbook: From Hand Pies to Hand Grenades, is a current best seller. *(HIS 436, PSY 363)*

Tom Ackerman—Associate Professor of BioEnglish
Mr. Ackerman had a fruitful career in HVAC repair, before finding his true passion: visceral fiction. Tom lives with his beloved thylacine Marisol, and, when not writing or teaching, works on expanding his collection of windup toys with mysterious pasts. See his many tweets at @TomSlackerman *(BIO 250, BIO 414, ENG 470, ENG 155)*

Steven Brandt—Professor of Internal and Interdimensional Medicine
Dr. Brandt received his doctorate at Blackwood University during a lunar eclipse. He presented detailed simulations of what would happen to a live human if dropped onto the surface of a neutron star. Due to the vividness of his visualizations and unfortunate similarity to people who went missing in the area of the university in the years leading up to his Ph.D., his thesis, the code, and related software remains sealed in the data vaults in the 6th sub-basement of the H.P. Lovecraft Memorial Library. *(CSC 044, MED 103)*

John Baltisberger, PhD, MoD, PrM—Dean of Nafallen University
Dr. Baltisberger attained his doctorate in metaphysics from Miskatonic Univerity in New England before moving to Texas to engage in the study of signs as read in the entrails of bigots. On top of running the most prestigious university of occult and divine studies in the United States, Dr. Baltisberger is the Publishing Editor of Madness Heart Press, and the Design Lead at Madness Heart Games. In his off time, Dr. Baltisberger enjoys screaming at flowers and dressing small mammals in alligator skin suits. You may find more of him at www.kaijupoet.com *(BUS 107, BUS 203, REL 101, REL 102, REL 138, REL 666, REL 777, REL 042)*

Professor **Matt Henshaw**, after acquiring advanced degrees from such institutions as Jakeshort University (Lower Leeds, Mass.), La Escuela Nueva de Medicina (Torgo, Argentina), and Harkendott University (Skillt, Norway), settled near the city of Crisp, TX with a charge from the Wise and Glorious Masters to establish Nafallen University. Along with other occult scholars and sage bedlamites, known and unknown to history, the school has grown and continues to grow, a rank pus-filled sore streaming into the surrounding county, and eventually, this cursed and blighted world.

Professor Henshaw invites you and compels you to learn all your pitiful mind can take in, and to use that knowledge to serve the Masters. Professor Henshaw may be summoned via the publisher of this course catalog or electronic mail to nafallen.university@gmail.com. If and when he traverses this pitiful physical plane next (some think he does not, and never did), he will be glad to make your acquaintance and find a place for you in the school, as student, as faculty, or as something else . . .

Additional Faculty:
Jan Libby—Orchestral Director and Professor of Combative Acoustic Studies *(EGR 401)*
Kathryn Reilly—Associate Professor of Discordant Screams *(BUS 102, COM 103, COM 312, ENG 101, ENG 103, ENG 104, BIO 312, ENT 101, ENT 102, HIS 102, HIS 302, MUS 201, PSY 301)*
Trevor Williamson—Professor of Missing Letters *(PHL 224, PHL 103, PHL 403)*

Made in the USA
Monee, IL
14 June 2022